THE POEM
AS PLANT

THE POEM AS PLANT

A Biological View of Goethe's Faust

By PETER SALM

The Press of
Case Western Reserve University
Cleveland & London
1971

Illustration on p. 26, courtesy Nationale Forschungs- und Gedenk-stätten der klassischen deutschen Literatur in Weimar. *Corpus der Goethezeichnungen*, VB (Leipzig, 1957), No. 86.

Grateful acknowledgment is made to the following: *The German Quarterly*, for permission to reproduce passages from my "Faust, Eros and Knowledge" (May 1966); *Germanic Review*, for permission to reproduce passages from my "Faust and Irony" (May 1965); Penguin Books, Ltd., for permission to reproduce passages from *Faust*, translated by Philip Wayne; Bantam Books, Inc., for permission to reproduce passages from my translation of *Faust*, first part.

For my boy Tony

A Note on the Translations

If the numerous quotations in the text were left untranslated the accessibility of the book would tend to remain rather sternly limited—unnecessarily so, I believe. It is intended, after all, not only for the specialist in German literature but also for those who have an interest in the *Faust* drama as world literature and in its relationship to Goethe's philosophy of science. Indeed, this study may be regarded as an exercise in criticism which avails itself of concepts and formulations carried over from natural science, idiosyncratic though Goethe's science may appear to be.

All German passages are therefore offered in translation. In the case of poetry and explicitly literary prose the original German text is given as well. Passages of discursive prose are generally given only in English because a lengthy dual presentation seemed cumbersome and unnecessary when only the sense was being discussed and when this could be adequately conveyed in translation. Those wishing to consult the original are in each case referred to its source.

For numerous lines from *Faust II*, I used Philip Wayne's translation; for certain passages from Goethe's *Iphigenia*, I chose Anna Swanwick's version, and for *Tasso* that of

Ben Kimpel and T. C. Duncan Eaves. The verses from *Faust I* were taken from my own previously published translation and the English in other passages is mine unless otherwise noted.

Contents

Introduction

During the planning and writing of this volume there
came insistently to my mind the image, in Goethe's *Faust*,
of an intricate organic harmony, of a shifting form, dis-
similar in outline from moment to moment but always
following the same principles of design. It was a concrete structure, inasmuch as it could be felt, apprehended,
and invoked, but it seemed elusive because it would not
be captured and secured by logic or demonstration. This
image did not present itself in response to a question, but
rather as a palpable reality, like a tree, which does not
answer a single question but which irrevocably exists.

It has often been shown that Goethe tended to think of
his literary works in biological rather than architectonic
terms. His youthful veneration of Shakespeare, his dab-
blings in alchemy and mysticism ripened into the mature
"organicism" of a superbly educated intellect. Whether
it was a problem in geology or a question of literary form,
Goethe's recourse was consistently a deep-seated faith in
the processes of organic growth in which each event appears as a summation of the past and as a seminal pattern
for the future. Such a pattern will change even in the act
of observation, not in a cause-and-effect sequence but
by way of a series of metamorphoses comprehensible only

through a kind of personal involvement that Goethe liked to call "higher contemplation" *(höhere Anschauung)* and "delicate empiricism" *(zarte Empirie).*

We are not yet far enough removed from Romanticism to be startled by Goethe's "organic" approach to literature; the Schlegel brothers in Germany and Coleridge in England provided the theoretical basis for a revaluation of literary norms in the direction of organicism. But we are ill prepared to cope with Goethe's natural philosophy which, as we shall see, is non-mathematical and, in a sense, non-theoretical. It is, after all, only *our* science which has brought about spectacular successes in technology. But Goethe was not interested in conceptual "conquest" of his environment. He sought insight as an enthralled participant in nature rather than as an objective observer. Human activity was inseparable from natural processes. Objective observation, therefore, or theoretical edifices based on these processes were illusory and misleading. A "fact" emerges at the intersection of emanations which flow from the phenomenon and from its observer. The refinement of such a vision of reality is an indispensable component of Goethean "higher contemplation" where all true insight into natural processes comes from a dynamic union between subject and object.

That Goethe's natural philosophy and his poetry have important common elements has been frequently pointed out by biographers and interpreters of his writings. But studies concerning this relationship have dealt primarily with detailed and explicit congruences rather than overall analogies. This has been especially true with respect to the *Faust* poem. Specific passages are sometimes singled out in order to deduce from them Goethe's views on natural science, for example, the lines in *Faust II* referring to the origin of the earth's physiognomy according to the contrasting theories of "Vulcanism" or "Neptunism."

Of greater significance, I feel, would be a structural analysis of major portions of *Faust*—and indeed of the total drama—and the ranging of this *Faust* structure alongside Goethe's "concrete idea" concerning certain basic natural phenomena, such as color or vegetative growth.

Among the dangers of assuming an overall Faustian unity is a natural tendency toward restrictiveness. It seems almost unavoidable that the elaboration of one structural metaphor should tend to exclude others which are also present. Recently, *Faust* scholars like Stuart Atkins have taken a pessimistic view of the usefulness of structural studies because "a feeling for large and complex aesthetic structures is simply not sufficiently common in our post-classical, fragmented and even schizoid age."[1]

Yet during the last few decades, structural approaches have become more frequent, and the interpretive issues raised by them more insistent. Recently, musical configurations in *Faust* were identified by Hermann Fähnrich, who discerned patterns analogous to leitmotiv, tonality, and Morzartian counterpoint, and concluded that the elements of music supply the building stones of the poem.[2]

While operatic moments and structures are undoubtedly and gloriously present in *Faust*, particularly in those parts written by the mature and aged poet, it is hard to believe that they constitute the chief structural element of the drama. The imagery in *Faust* will not support it; Goethe's life and relative lack of musical acumen contradict it. It is well to note that late in his life Goethe confessed to his composer friend Zelter, "Musically deaf and dumb, though a good listener, I convert my musical experiences into words and concepts. I know well enough that this leaves me deprived of one third of life; but one must learn to accommodate oneself" (Goethe to Zelter, May 2, 1820).

Among the most fruitful attempts toward arriving at a grasp of the total Faust drama are those rooted in a recognition of the enormous role of natural science in Goethe's life and poetry. The first to apply systematically Goethe's scientific concepts to a number of scenes in *Faust* was Wilhelm Herz.[3] His method was an important departure into a new interpretative dimension, and as a result, such myths as the "Mothers" and scenes like Faust's final ascension could be interpreted through Goethe's natural philosophy as well as through their immediate poetic context.

Important studies aimed at developing a conceptual framework for the application of the principles of Goethe's plant morphology to his poetry were undertaken only during the last few decades. Günther Müller's initial investigation of 1944[4] was soon followed by Horst Oppel's partisan advocacy of the adoption of a Goethe-oriented morphological structuralism for all literature, in place of the traditional aesthetic norms.[5] More recently, L. A. Willoughby was successful in developing analogies between Goethe's science and some of his poetry in terms of "mirror reflection" and "heightening." In an essay on *Faust* the author sought to probe beneath the verbal surface by "exploring the relations between words," on the assumption that such explorations, if conducted with controlled imagination, "must lead to the most inward systems of the whole organism."[6] Words like *Welt, Brust,* and *Busen* are shown in their contextual patterns and nuances of meaning. An intricate web of interrelationships can thus be discerned and adduced as convincing evidence for an overall verbal unity which reflects important aspects of Goethe's vision of a living organism.

Helmut Rehder provides an illuminating analysis of frequent four-fold patterns in the drama, often associated with stages of "heightening." Rehder sees these patterns as competing and interacting with triadic structures, and rightly warns against accepting too static a concept of any particular structure because "a growing plant knows of no stages; neither does the entelechy . . . which is seen passing through the realm of [becoming] and incrementation."[7]

A study of vegetation symbols leads Heinz Politzer, almost incidentally, to a structural aperçu similar to Rehder's: "Goethe's *Faust* not only grew like a tree during the better part of his life, but is also a very symmetrical composition."[8]

The subject of this study is the relationship between *Faust* and the Goethean vision of a plant. I owe something to all those who have pointed out this special analogy between nature and poetry, but I am especially indebted to those who have begun to draw the consequences of the assumption that Goethean science could operate as a powerful tool for a deepened understanding of his imaginative writings. I have come to believe that the interpretive possibilities of this method are considerable, and I expect that continuing explorations in this relatively new direction will yield interesting results.

The analogy between poetry and nature is here explored on the basis of three principles: "polarity," "metamorphosis," and "heightening." An analysis of the complicated interplay between them seems to open the way to a special appreciation of the dynamics of the *Faust* poem.

We are well acquainted with numerous Goethean metaphors surrounding the proto-phenomenon of "polarity." In the field of color theory it may appear as darkness and light, in biology as spiral or vertical growth tendencies. In the fable and structure of *Faust*, polarity may appear as the "two souls" in Faust's breast, as the struggle between Faust and Mephistopheles, or as the contest between cold reason and glowing emotion. Polarity invades content and form, language and style. For example, it can effectively function within a mode traditionally known as irony, inasmuch as irony is a play with opposite possibilities in language, style, and story.

"Metamorphosis" is shown as a phenomenon in biology and optics in order to determine whether it is related or analogous to those structural elements in *Faust* which have come to be known as "mirror reflections," and above all whether metamophosis is linked, as it is in Goethean "nature," to the principles of Faustian "heightening" or intensification. In a plant, heightening in this sense refers to the upward development leading to the flowering stage. In Goethe's color theory it is a movement through the "lesser" colors of yellow and blue toward the regal *purpur*, or red. Metamorphosis and heightening in *Faust* will be sought in the stages of the hero's development, as well as in the progressive changes in the drama's style and tempo. Because it is not possible to speak of the effective presence of metamorphosis without also referring to a particular stage in the process of heightening, the two principles are discussed jointly in a single chapter. The goal here and elsewhere in this book is not completeness, not a gathering of all instances, but rather an illumination of those qualities and functions which can be seen to give life to overall structural patterns.

All three principles, however, are subject to and dependent upon the pervasive force of eros. Eros in *Faust* is like a magnet drawing all matter and spirit toward itself. It refines lust to love and touches even gross language and rhythms with a hint of sublime poetry. One chapter is devoted to its protean manifestations and to its role in the drama's peculiar dynamics.

The first part of the book deals with Goethe's science, specifically with his plant morphology and color theory. It is an attempt to develop Goethe's way of seeing and responding to his environment, without explicitly dwelling on the categories of metamophosis, polarity, heightening, and eros. These will emerge naturally, it is hoped, even in the absence of meticulous labeling. In the second part entitled "Morphology and *Faust*," each of these categories or principles is discussed in a separate section emphasizing how those ideas introduced in the first part can influence a fresh interpretation of *Faust*.

If the analogy can be sustained between the ruling patterns in Goethe's perception of physical nature and the overall morphology of *Faust*, then the immense mass of the composition can be seen as a complex and coherent whole. The work of the positivist scholars who with great diligence and acumen worked out the chronology of *Faust's* composition over fifty-eight or sixty years of Goethe's life will thereby certainly not be out of date. It will always be an essential aid to interpretation. But the great length of time needed for the composition of *Faust* must not serve as a mitigating circumstance for Goethe's supposed sins against unity and coherence, nor should it be necessary to adduce, in defense of the difficulties in *Faust II*, the aloofness or wrongheadedness of an old man. References to Goethe's *Altersstil* have in the past not always been merely descriptive. Out of respect for a great man's old age we are sometimes asked to make allowances for deficiences in continuity and for unresolvable ambiguities.

Goethe's creative spirit was peculiarly unified, whether it dwelt upon the processes of nature or upon the making of poetry. The need and artistic consummation of such a synthesis of divergent sensibilities can be seen as one of the attributes of Romanticism, and indeed in a European context Goethe is generally regarded as a Romantic poet. But more than a metaphysical convergence in infinity between natural philosophy and poetry is at stake in *Faust*. Applied broadly enough such congruences are not confined to Romanticism but exist between all great poetry and all great scientific structures. We can agree with Santayana when he writes:

> No one can reach insight who has not enlarged his mind and tamed his heart. A philosopher who attains it is, for the moment, a poet. And a poet who turns his practiced and passionate imagination on the order of all things, or on anything in the light of the whole, is for that moment a philosopher.[9]

What is peculiar to *Faust* is that beyond some general affinities between poetry and natural philosophy it is closely structured in analogy to a dynamic vision of vegetative life. An interpretation of *Faust* as a drama must take into account Goethe's profound preoccupation with natural science. Such an expanded view will yield important benefits; for example, the apparent contradiction between Faust's final salvation and the subtitle "a tragedy" can then be reexamined in a new light. Goethe's often debated avoidance of tragedy in the Aristotelean sense takes on greater plausibility than before, once his special scientific norms are rigorously and consistently applied.

Goethe's lengthy scientific tracts have not yet been sufficiently exploited for such interpretive studies. Their structure and their doctrine were approached with different eyes and with more skepticism than his poetic writings. Doubts concerning the validity of Goethe's scientific views became doubts about their relevance to his poetry. As a result, literary criticism of *Faust* that takes into account the full scope of Goethe's science is rare and has remained somewhat obscure. I have become convinced in the course of this study that to gain access, no matter how tentative and ephemeral, to the singleness of Goethe's vision, which perhaps more than ever before or since fused abstract theory with vital experience, is worth a great deal of effort.

NOTES

[1]"The Interpretation of Goethe's *Faust* Since 1958," *Orbis Litterarum* XX (1965), p. 266. See also the condensation of the above article in "Studies of Goethe's *Faust* Since 1959," *The German Quarterly* XXXIX (May, 1966), p. 310.

[2]Hermann Fähnrich, "Goethes Musikanschauung in seiner Fausttragödie—die Erfüllung and Vollendung seiner Opernreform," *Jahrbuch der Goethe-Gesellschaft* XXV (1963), pp. 250–63.

[3]*Goethes Naturphilosophie in Faust* (Berlin, 1913). See also *Natur und Geist in Goethes Faust* (Frankfurt, 1931).

[4]"Die Gestaltfrage in der Literaturwissenschaft und Goethes Morphologie," *Die Gestalt*, (Halle a/S, 1944), Heft 13. Not available to me at this writing.

[5]"As a first step it will be necessary to leave behind the aesthetic norms of structure and instead view literary structure as a manifestation of life, of all-encompassing nature" (*Mor-*

phologische Naturwissenschaft. Goethes Ansicht und Methode [Mainz, 1947], p. 30).

[6]Elizabeth M. Wilkinson and L. A. Willoughby, *Goethe, Poet and Thinker* (New York, 1962), p. 99ff.

[7]Helmut Rehder, "Tetradic Structure in Goethe's *Faust*," *The Germanic Review* XXXVIII (January, 1963), p. 64.

[8]From "The Tree of Knowledge and the Sin of Science: Vegetarian Symbols in Goethe's *Faust*," in *Aspects of the Eighteenth Century*, Earl R. Wasserman, ed. (Baltimore, 1965), p. 296.

[9]*Three Philosophical Poets*, 8th ed. (Cambridge, 1947), pp. 10–11.

I · NATURE AS ORGANISM

1 • General Outlook

Goethe's unremitting attempts at understanding and conceptualizing natural phenomena have never, to my knowledge, been thought to have adversely affected his activities as a poet; his most enthusiastic partisans bestowed on him such titles as "the last universal genius" or "the last Renaissance man." Yet conversely, Goethe's reputation as a poet, as well as his unorthodox experimental procedures, gave his scientific endeavors the deadly stigma of dilettantism. Goethe refused to put his faith in the rigorous application of mathematical logic to natural phenomena, a method which had after all yielded the great theoretical edifices of Copernicus, Kepler, and Newton. He could not fragment his sensibilities; rather, by directing his inquiry toward the relationship between self and nature, subject and object, he attempted to formulate a synthesis —as valid for poets as for natural philosophers—that would reveal the phenomenal world undiluted by abstractions. And undoubtedly, Goethe's way of encompassing complexities and contradictory coherences was the way of poetry.

Poetry was for him not a selection of impressions from nature, nor was it a mirror to nature. Rather than imitate, art should *compete* with nature's processes, and great art, though illuminated by nature, should transcend it. Art is a man-made natural phenomenon, a heightened analogy, informed by the precise structure of the imagination. A poem is both fact and meaning, object and subject, activity as well as awareness, natural phenomenon as well as experiment—and it is such paradoxical correspondences in Goethe which are in need of critical examination. They are too real to be dismissed as "mere" poetic metaphors.

It is likely that Goethe will always be known as a great poet rather than a great scientist, though it is difficult to say which title he would have preferred. Universally regarded as Germany's, perhaps Europe's, greatest poet since Shakespeare, he enjoyed a full measure of recognition during his long life. But very few looked upon Goethe with equal awe as a man of science. His war on Newton's *Opticks* in particular was wholly unsuccessful and was dismissed as an amateurish effort.

He was hypersensitive in matters touching on his scientific accomplishments. Eckermann, his faithful amanuensis, reported that, when he expressed with the utmost tact certain doubts about details of the *Theory of Color*, Goethe turned on him saying, "You are a heretic just like the others, for you are not the first to deviate from me" (March 19, 1829). Other statements made by the aged Goethe in a more serene mood can be taken more seriously:

> I don't flatter myself in the least for all I have accomplished as a poet. Some of my contemporaries have been fine poets; even finer poets have preceded me and there will be others after me. However, that I am the only one in my century who knows the truth in the difficult field of Color Theory, that is a fact concerning which I take some pride; hence, I have an awareness of superiority over many [March 19, 1829].

And it is a sense of quiet assurance which emanates from his well-known words to Eckermann, spoken a year before his death: "My theory of colors is as old as the world and in the long run cannot be denied or put out of the way" (March 18, 1831).

It would seem then that a reassessment of Goethe's scientific writings would be justifiable, if only on the ground that a great mind expended so much time and energy in their production. One can reject Goethe's theory of color and his plant morphology, but in arriving at a judgment we are at least bound to gain a deepened understanding of the slant and style of Goethe's mind, which continues to be of vital significance.

No attempt will be made in this study either to enhance or to derogate Goethe's stature as a scientist or natural philosopher. We will merely note in passing that this question has been and still is the subject of lively controversy.

We should remember that academic science—the "guild," as Goethe called it—rejected his scientific philosophy and methods. Flushed with the great victories of mathematical and deterministic explanations of natural phenomena, the scientific community of the nineteenth century showed little patience with Goethe's mistrust of mathematical analysis applied to the processes of nature.

There was, however, a sprinkling of eminent men who thought highly of his contributions to biology, for example, Auguste de Saint-Hilaire, whose widely accepted textbook *Leçons de Botanique* (1841) contains many references to Goethe's work on morphology. The famous German traveler and explorer Alexander von Humboldt (1769–1859) acknowledged his debt to Goethe on many occasions and dedicated to him his first book on plant geography, the results of his travels to Central and South America.

Throughout the nineteenth century and to this day there has been a question as to whether Goethe should be taken seriously as a scientific thinker. Certainly those who regard the applicability of scientific principles to technology as proof of the validity of such principles could have no use for Goethe's views. The problem of the relationship between subject and object, between observer and the observed phenomena, which so profoundly preoccupied Goethe, was of little importance to the new science, whose victorious march through laboratories and factories had become indispensable to modern civilization.

Among modern scientific thinkers, the physiologist Charles Sherrington[1] and the historian of science Charles C. Gillispie[2] sternly reject Goethe's methods as lacking in scientific value, while the physicist Werner Heisenberg[3] and the biologist Agnes Arbor[4] not only acknowledge Goethe's importance to science, but are evidently inspired and influenced by him. Sherrington's evaluation unfortunately suffers from a narrowly professional approach; he judges Goethe almost entirely on whether his discoveries have in our own day been accepted or rejected. By such a criterion Goethe fares very poorly, especially since Sherrington even discredits Goethe's independent discovery of the intermaxillary bone in the human skull, on the ground that the French biologist Vicq d'Azur had discovered it several years earlier. Sherrington does not recognize the fundamental challenge which Goethe posed to the mechanistic science of his era and fails to see in that challenge any implications for modern scientific thought. Gillispie, whose rejection is based on Goethe's "romanticism" and lack of objectivity, brilliantly develops the notion that science was able to advance to its present high level only by excluding sense organs as judges of natural phenomena. Gillispie is convinced that only by sacrificing the subjective element has science progressed to the status of an objective discipline.

The question of Goethe's place in science has not received a final answer—evidence, perhaps, of an uncertainty which reflects our own philosophical quandary about the relationship between science and nature. Generally speaking, however, biologists acknowledge Goethe as a founder and inspirer of "idealistic morphology,"[5] while most physicists tend to shrug him off as a brilliant dilettante. Goethe's work in morphology was considered an advance, though not a revolutionary one. In the concluding paragraph of an essay written in 1795, Goethe himself denies any revolutionary intentions in the field of botany: "[My morphology] has the great advantage that it consists of elements which are generally recognized, that it is not in contention with any other view, that it need not displace anything to make room for itself . . ."[6]

On the other hand, Goethe's futile and wrong-headed critique of Newton's *Opticks* was a direct assault on a mighty fortress of mathematical thought and served to militate against his stature as a man of science, even though his *Theory of Color* was not to remain without its adherents. Adolph Bernays, for example, concluded that Goethe never really spoke of colors as physical phenomena but rather as sense impressions.[7] Therefore, according to Bernays, it was in the field of physiological colors that Goethe made an important contribution and in fact anticipated modern experiments by more than a century. Consequently there were really no grounds for controversy between Goethe and Newton, their theories being complementary rather than mutually exclusive. Bernays' facile way of composing the quarrel hardly touches the core of the matter, for far from being concerned with the limits of different scientific disciplines, the issue concerned the structure of knowledge itself. It is evident that Goethe would not have been satisfied with having his *Theory of Color* regarded merely as a contribution to physiology; he specifically stated that he considered Newton to be wholly mistaken and that he himself was aiming to break down his already crumbling castle.[8]

Similarly, a series of color experiments conducted by Edwin H. Land[9] provisionally indicate a far more autonomous role of the human eye with respect to color than had previously been supposed. Land's experiments would largely justify the prominent role which Goethe accorded to human physiology in color perception. Yet by regarding color as "deeds of light" rather than "deeds of the eye," Goethe was in error from the point of view of modern science.[10]

Clearly, Goethe's science can not be regarded merely as a poet's eccentricity.[11] However, the nature and scope of the present investigation does not call for an assessment of the validity or importance of Goethe's philosophy of science today. I intend rather to avail myself of that considerable portion of Goethe's life which was devoted to the systematic observation of natural phenomena, so that a tool may be developed for the interpretation of his poetic writings and especially of his *Faust* poem. If it were possible, for example, to show how *Faust* partakes in several essential ways of Goethe's view of nature, then one might with greater confidence than heretofore use his pronouncements in one area to illuminate their counterpart in another. Proliferating and vague analogies would then be avoided and at the same time a new interpretative tool could be put to the test. The task of relating the two directions of Goethe's endeavors—poetry and science—to each other, is made somewhat more difficult by the divided sensibilities of our own post-Copernican age. The new physical cosmos is no longer accessible to the poetic imagination as it had been during the Renaissance when the ancient basic stuffs still pervaded the world, and the dominance of one or the other "humor" could make a man's temperament melancholic, phlegmatic, or choleric. Thus the words of Mark Antony about Brutus were descriptive rather than metaphorical:

> His life was gentle, and the elements
> So mix'd in him that nature might stand up
> And say to all the world, "This was a man."

But with Francis Bacon, Shakespeare's image became an illusion and, if taken seriously, a harmful idol:

> Nay, it is not credible, till it be opened, what a number of fictions and fancies the similitude of human actions and arts, together with the making of man *communis mensura,* have brought into natural philosophy; not much better than the heresy of the Anthropomorphites bred in the cells of gross and solitary monks, and the opinion of Epicurus, answerable to the same heathenism, who supposed the Gods to be of human shape.[12]

Marjorie Nicolson has shown how science became proudly prosaic and how the "Chain of Being" of the old world was reduced to the level of a pleasant figure of speech.[13]

A target of Goethe's persistent attack was the inclination by scientists to develop theories about contingent natural phenomena, i.e., to connect specific observations in logical or causative sequences. To Goethe, such theories seemed entirely unwarranted, apt to lead to subjective errors, and tantamount to oversimplification or even falsification of the phenomenon under observation: "Theories are usually overhasty fabrications of an impatient mind which would like to do away with phenomena and consequently will inject pictures, concepts, or even just words in their place."[14] This was written about 1823, when Goethe had passed into the last decade of his long life. But at the age of twenty-five he had expressed the same view in an entirely different context in *Werther*. The limitations imposed on Werther by his human condition are the correlate of his imperious need for absolutes. Werther writes to his friend Wilhelm (letter of May 22):

> When I am faced with the restrictions which incarcerate man's dynamic and questing powers; when I see how all activity merely serves to satisfy needs which in turn have no purpose except to prolong our miserable existence, and then [when I see] that any calmness with respect to certain points of inquiry is merely a dreamy resignation while we cover the walls of our imprisonment with gay figures and bright vistas—all this, Wilhelm, makes me silent—I descend into my own self and find a world.

It is not too farfetched to conclude that the "bright views" and "gay figures" on the walls in *Werther* became "impatient" hypotheses and theories for the older Goethe.

10

Goethe thought mathematics and logical analysis to be extraneous to the character of natural phenomena whose secrets they were not capable of unveiling. Several maxims incorporated in Goethe's *Notebooks on Natural Science* may serve here to clarify the tenor of the attack on the kind of thinking which was dominating the minds of the scientific establishment:

> Hypotheses are cradle songs with which the teacher lulls his pupils. . . .[15]

> What is exact in mathematics but its own exactitude?[16]

> Mathematics cannot dispose of prejudices; it can neither prevent obstinacy nor mitigate factionalism. It is impotent in all ethical matters.[17]

Goethe practiced, described, and continuously urged a radically different approach to nature, in which the phenomenon was not to be broken down into its individual components but perceived instead in its totality. Factuality *is* theory and should not be further fragmented:

> The highest boon would be to understand that all facts are already theory. The blue of the sky reveals to us the basic chromatic laws. If we would only stop looking for things behind the phenomena; they themselves are the theory.[18]

It appeared to Goethe that theories were based on preconceived "unnatural" notions, whereas a mature and receptive mind could absorb the totality of the relationship existing between the subjective and objective aspects of a given event. Human beings adjust to their environment in such a manner that their sense organs are able to perceive only those phenomena to which these organs bear a resemblance or to which they have become adapted. Thus in the introduction to his *Theory of Color* he writes, referring indirectly to a principle enunciated in the third century A.D. by Plotinus:[19]

> The eye owes its existence to light. Out of indifferent, auxiliary animal organisms light summons forth an organ to be its peer; and thus the eye is informed by light and formed for light so that the inward light may issue forth to confront its external counterpart.[20]

It was absurd to proclaim, Goethe felt, that the color white was composed of all the colors of the spectrum. Such a notion would be at odds with the testimony of the senses. What is more, color should be described not as an isolated phenomenon but as one that results from an encounter between the observer and the observed.

Nor was mathematical induction capable of revealing the nature of light and color. While there was room in Goethe's doctrine for scientific experiments, they could be useful only if conducted in the proper manner. Isolated experiments could be and had been employed to prove almost anything, as long as they could be made to fit into some mathematical or logical scheme. According to Goethe, this was precisely the error at the bottom of Newton's color theory, for it was Newton who had erected his entire theoretical edifice on three isolated experiments.[21] While Newton regarded colors as objectively and physically inherent in light, Goethe insisted that they were the result of a complicated though knowable reciprocity between the observer and the phenomenon of light. Only a great cluster of interrelated and contiguous experiments could approximate and parallel the natural context. To isolate a phenomenon was tantamount to falsifying it, but in combination experiments could reveal the manifold connections between the phenomenon, nature, and the observing self. There is a higher principle underlying such a series which could come to light so long as the results of such experiments were not prejudged by hasty hypotheses.[22]

Goethe's aversion to isolating scientific experiments finds its modern echo in the writings of the physicist Werner Heisenberg:

> Natural science no longer deals with the world which directly presents itself to us, but with the dark background of this world which is brought to light by our experiments—and to that extent we touch on the insuperable limits of human knowledge. From this development it can be seen that Goethe's struggle against the physicists' color theory must still be carried out today on a broadened front.[23]

and of the literary scholar Erich Heller:

> The dangers threatening modern science cannot be averted by more and more experimenting, for our complicated experiments have no longer anything to do with nature in her own right, but with nature changed and transformed by our own cognitive activity.[24]

What was Goethe's solution to the dilemma? Experiments were necessary and desirable for anyone striving to see into the workings of nature, but such experiments would inevitably involve a rearranging and to some extent a falsification of nature. Moreover, how was one to draw conclusions from such experiments without falling into the trap of constructing hasty and unwarranted hypotheses? Here Goethe offers a new principle which seems strange to modern positivistic habits. According to this principle—which might be characterized as one of aesthetic and ethical maturity, but which defies further definition—insights into the workings of nature could be attained only by highly developed individuals whose particular technical skills would be secondary to a basic, infinitely refined sensibility. In 1779 Goethe wrote; "There exists a delicate empiricism which aims for a most intimate identity with the object and thus becomes the actual and proper theory. However, such heightening of spiritual capacity belongs to a highly civilized epoch."[25] This would point to a way of combining and merging "experience" and "idea" where the idea is not an abstraction but a condensation or crystallization of experimental data. Again and again Goethe warns against imposing a preconceived structure upon nature merely for the sake of warding off an irrational chaos: "A special slant of mind is required to grasp shapeless reality in its own terms, and this is to be distinguished from brain-spun phantoms which, to be sure, importune us with a certain reality of their own."[26]

Significantly, Goethe designates reality as "shapeless," *gestaltlos*, and indicates that the deepest perception of such reality comes not through defining and limiting— this would be part and parcel of the brain-spun phantoms *(Hirngespinste)*—but through apprehending it in its own terms.

Goethe refused to acknowledge form as a separate reality. A plant, he maintained, exists in its substance as well as in its form. Neither mode of existence may be isolated without destroying the living essence of the other. Moreover, Goethe held that the category of form exists only as a principle of communion between subject and object.

As early as 1775 he wrote in his diary: "Every form, no matter how deeply felt, has something untrue about it; yet once and for all it is the lens through which the sacred shafts of nature's expanse are gathered up in a fiery point for man's heart to behold."[27]

Goethe, whose life was devoted to the creation, vision, and perception of form, refers to this category of the mind as something illusory—an astounding statement to come from a poet who was also one of the founders of comparative morphology.

To be meaningful, form had to be found within the larger context of the "concrete idea" of an object or a phenomenon, of which form itself would be only one of several constituents; "time," "growth," and "value" would be others.

The account of Goethe's first encounter with Friedrich Schiller in Jena may serve to set off his view of the "idea" against Schiller's more truly Platonic notion. In Goethe's notebooks covering the year 1794 we read:

> Schiller and I arrived at his house; I was drawn inside by the conversation; I gave a lively presentation of the metamorphosis of plants and by means of a few characteristic strokes of the pen conjured up before his eyes a symbolic plant. He listened and looked upon all that with great interest and sharp comprehension; but when I had finished he shook his head and said: "That is not experience; it is an idea!" I was taken aback and felt some annoyance: for the issue which divided us was hereby precisely drawn . . . but I pulled myself together and replied: "I am much gratified to know that I have ideas without knowing it, and can even see them with my eyes. . . ."[28]

This initial personal encounter with Schiller was the beginning of their celebrated friendship. Their courteous though profound disagreement brought home to Goethe the necessity of justifying and philosophically buttressing an article of faith which had been of central importance to his poetic and scientific outlook. A connecting link between an abstract idea and specific experimental data had to be found, for the highest and most valuable moments of creative consciousness were precisely the ones in which the two coincided. Only the "exact imagination," applied by the creator of poetry as well as by the reader, can bridge the gap and come face to face with what today we are apt to call the "Concrete Universal."[29]

In 1820, Goethe wrote that through poetry alone could one escape the madness which would inevitably result from attempts to combine concept and experience.[30] When in 1787 he had come upon the notion of the *Urpflanze* ("archetypal plant") it produced in him an almost religious excitement, to which a letter to Frau von Stein in 1787 gives testimony.[31] But after his encounter with Schiller he wrote with a degree of skepticism: "Theory and experience (phenomena) are in steady conflict with one another—whatever union between them can be effected by reflection is illusory; only action can unite them.[32] The archetypal plant cannot be grasped by mere contemplation, but is encountered in rare moments only by those who know how to unite concept and experience through "activity" *(Handeln).* The nature of such activity, difficult to define, is nevertheless so central to Goethe's outlook that it comes close to being an analogy to life itself. Describing the "higher levels" of existence he writes in 1823: "And so I reiterate my own view, that on these higher levels one cannot know but must act, just as in play one needs to know very little and achievement is all."[33]

A Goethean "idea" then is concrete and inherent in the phenomenon. It is at once particular and universal, momentary and perennial, and its apprehension is possible only through "action." It exists in itself, but is also symbol and analogue for all existence. "Whatever exists is an analogue to all other existence."[34] Moreover to a fully developed empirical sense a phenomenon always "is" what it appears to be. Goethe's natural science, therefore, avoids abstractions and theoretical systems, as well as the alienation from sensible nature which Werner Heisenberg perceives and deplores in modern science and which Charles C. Gillispie asserts is the price which we must pay for scientific penetration of our environment.

In Kant's *Critique of Judgment* Goethe found confirmation of his own conviction that natural science and poetry are subject to the same category of the mind, in spite of the differences between the tools and methods of the scientist and the artist. He was grateful to be given the theoretical support for his own view that nature, like art, is essentially devoid of moral purposes:

> My aversion to final causes was now regulated and justified; I could clearly differentiate between goals and effects; I also understood why these were often confused in the mind. I was pleased to realize that poetry [*Dichtkunst*] and comparative natural science were closely related, inasmuch as they both are subject to the same norms and judgment.[35]

By the time Goethe wrote these words (1820) he had long since achieved maturity both as a poet and as a natural philosopher; thus his renewed attraction to Kant's philosophy between 1817 and 1820 could not have changed his views in any fundamental way. One can sense his joy, however, in reading how he saw his own views reflected in the carefully constructed intellectual edifice of a great and systematic philosopher.

Goethe thought of art as a heightened analogy of nature, differing profoundly from it, but being at the same time nature's distillation and symbol. The eternal forms and processes of nature, for example, the archetypal plant, while capable of evoking concrete symbols in the mind's eye could not be represented by a two- or three-dimensional model, because such a model would encompass neither time nor continuous change. Goethe's archetypal plant, for example, is a concrete version of an idea which subsumes an infinite variety of "leafy" forms in an infinity of moments: forms in time rather than forms in space. In the introduction to a group of essays on morphology (1817) Goethe writes:

> If we wish to introduce a morphology, we must not speak of form [*Gestalt*]; but rather, whenever we use the word, think of an idea, a concept, or something fixed for only the briefest moment.
>
> That which is formed is promptly re-formed, and if we expect to achieve any kind of vital contemplation [*Anschauung*] of Nature, we must keep ourselves flexible and malleable, according to the example with which she precedes us.[36]

Certain resemblances between Goethe's natural science and his poetry have long been taken for granted, but the extent and scope of such resemblances have not yet been fully surveyed. Of Goethe's works, *Faust* offers by far the richest possibilities for such a survey; a kind of "unified field theory" might be the final goal. If it is possible to show that the essential Goethean "grammar" of organic nature corresponds to the main structural features of *Faust*, then an important argument in support of the poem's unity will have been made. Stylistic, thematic, and structural congruences ought then to be classified under the general heading of "organic unity," a term which, acquiring demonstrable relevance, could no longer be regarded merely as a fanciful metaphor or a desperate escape from a critical cul-de-sac.

The quest for organic unity gave a decisive character to Goethe's early intellectual and emotional life. He sought to reconcile opposites in the phenomonological realm as well as in mutually exclusive modes of thought. In recapitulating his experience of perceiving the archetypal plant in Palermo, he wrote, while in Rome three months later:

> Forward and backward the plant is forever only leaf, so inseparably joined to its future seed that one may not think one without the other. To grasp such a concept, to cope with it, to detect it in nature, is a task which carries with it an aching sweetness.[37]

Whether this concept of the archetype was "experience" or "concept" could not finally be resolved during the friendly confrontation between Goethe and Schiller, but the scope of the problem becomes apparent in the following:

> Reason cannot unite that which the senses delivered to it separately, and so the quarrel between sense perception and abstraction remains forever unresolved.
>
> Hence we take some pleasure in making good our escape into poetry. . . .[38]

It is clear, however, that the discovery of the "visible

idea" in Palermo on April 17, 1787 was a turning point which decisively affected Goethe's creative endeavors in natural science and poetry.[39] In natural science he extended his discovery of the archetypal plant to the "type" in the animal kingdom. Whereas the *ur*-form for dicotyledenous annual plants was the leaf, the vertebra was the basic design for the bone structure of mammals. However, the most concrete and transparent realization of Goethe's vision in Palermo was reserved for his poetry, most particularly his *Faust*.

In furtherance of our discussion, we shall concentrate on Goethe's two major scientific works, the *Metamorphosis of Plants*, first published in 1790, and the *Theory of Color*, which appeared in 1810. It will be shown, once the main ideas have been absorbed, how both works are aspects of the same fundamental vision—which is shaped in accordance with the three cardinal principles of polarity, metamorphosis, and heightening, all under the aegis of eros.

NOTES

[1]Charles Sherrington, *Goethe on Nature and Science,* 2nd ed. (Cambridge, 1949).

[2]Charles C. Gillispie, *The Edge of Objectivity: An Essay in the History of Scientific Ideas* (Princeton, 1960).

[3]Werner Heisenberg, *Wandlungen in den Grundlagen der Naturwissenschaft* (Zurich, 1947); also, "Das Naturbild Goethes und die technisch-naturwissenschaftliche Welt," *Jahrbuch der Goethe-Gesellschaft* XXIX (1967), pp. 27–42.

[4]Agnes Arbor, "Goethe's Botany," *Chronica Botanica* X: 2 (1946).

[5]An expression coined by E. Radl in his *Geschichte der biologischen Theorien in der Neuzeit* (Leipzig, 1909) and adopted by Adolf Naef in his important work *Idealistische Morphologie*

und Philogenetik. Zur Methode der systematischen Morphologie (Jena, 1919).

[6]"Betrachtung über Morphologie überhaupt," *Jubiläumsausgabe*, ed. E. v. d. Hellen, 40 vols. (Stuttgart and Berlin, 1902–12) XXXIX, p. 137. Hereafter referred to as *Jubiläums.*

[7]"Zur Frage des Lichtsinns," *Dialectica* (October, 1949), pp. 236–41.

[8]Cf. *Jubiläums.* XL, pp. 64–65.

[9]"Experiments in Color Vision," *Scientific American* (May, 1959), pp. 84–99.

[10]See also the extensive footnote to Andreas B. Wachsmuth's "Goethes Farbenlehre und ihre Bedeutung für seine Dichtung und Weltanschauung," *Jahrbuch der Goethe-Gesellschaft* XXI (1959), pp. 92–93.

[11]Ernst Cassirer, for one, found his epistemology to be flawless and acknowledged that modern morphological thinking owed a great deal to him: "Only in the last few decades has there come a change. Science has been gradually learning to see Goethe's fundamental concepts with his own eyes, instead of measuring them by the standards of others" (Ernst Cassirer, *The Problem of Knowledge, Philosophy, History and Science since Hegel* [New Haven, 1950], p. 145).

[12]*The Advancement of Learning* (1651), G. W. Kitchin, ed. (London, 1915), chap. XIV, par. 9.

[13]Marjorie Hope Nicolson, *The Breaking of the Circle* (Evanston, Ill., 1950).

[14]*Jubiläums.* XXXIX, p. 64.

[15]Ibid., p. 73.

[16]Ibid., p. 76.

[17]Ibid., p. 77.

[18]Ibid., p. 72.

[19]See Plotinus, *Enneads*, V, 8, 1.

[20]*Hamburger Ausgabe*, ed. Erich Trunz, 3rd ed. (Hamburg, 1956), XIII, p. 323. Hereafter referred to as *Hamb. Ausg.*

[21]Cf. "Geschichte der Farbenlehre," *Hamb. Ausg.* XIV, p. 157.

[22]Cf Goethe's essay "Der Versuch als Vermittler von Objekt und Subjekt" (1792).

[23]*Wandlungen in den Grundlagen der Naturwissenschaft* (Zurich, 1947), p. 65.

[24]*The Disinherited Mind* (New York, 1959), p. 33.

[25]*Jubiläums.* XXXIX, p. 70.

[26]Ibid., p. 74.

[27]*Jubiläums.* XXXVI, p. 116.

[28]*Jubiläums.* XXX, p. 391.

[29]See W. K. Wimsatt, *The Verbal Icon, Studies in the Meaning of Poetry,* 2nd ed. (New York, 1958), pp. 69–83.

[30]Cf. quotation p. 19.

[31]See p. 105.

[32]*Jubiläums.* XXXIX, p. 115.

[33]Ibid., p. 61. The decisive influence of Friedrich W. Schelling in the matter of "activity" is attested by the following notes Goethe jotted down summarizing his reading of Schelling's philsophy of nature: "Unbedingtheit der Natur, das Unbedingte ist das *Sein.* Das Seinselbst ist das Konstruieren selbst. Das Sein ist die Tätigkeit. Die Natur wird als schlechthin tätig angesehen. Wie erscheint uns denn die Natur? Absolute Tätigkeit durch ein unendliches Produkt darstellbar. Möglichkeit der Darstellung des Unendlichen im Endlichen. Das empirische. Unendliche. Tätigkeit, die ins Unendliche fort gehemmt ist" (*Gedenkausgabe,* XVII, p. 709).

[34]*Jubiläums.* XXXIX, p. 68.

[35]"Einwirkung der neueren Philosophie," *Jubiläums.* XXXIX, p. 31.

[36]*Jubiläums.* XXXIX, p. 252.

[37]*Italienische Reise* (May 17, 1787).

[38]"Bedenken und Ergebung," *Jubiläums.* XXXIV, p. 35.

[39]Ernst Jockers recognizes essentially three phases of Goethe's morphology "which is itself subject to metamorphosis": Suchen des Gesetzes (1776–86), Finden des Gesetzes (1786–94), Verfestigung und Verhärtung im Gesetz (1795–1805). The "finding of the law" corresponds closely to the year 1787, deemed important also from our point of view. ("Morphologie und Klassik Goethes," in *Goethe und die Wissenschaft* [Frankfurt/M, 1951].)

2 · *Plant Morphology*

Goethe's deep and productive involvement in the natural sciences began modestly enough with an exposure to anatomy and osteology. Most of his dinner companions during his university days in Leipzig and Strasbourg were medical students whose jargon he quickly acquired. As early as 1775 he contributed to Johann Caspar Lavater's *Fragments in Physiognomy*,[1] most notably an essay on animal skulls. But he soon left behind his association with craniology and this protestant Swiss preacher and immensely popular charlatan character analyst. In 1781 he went to Jena to attend the famed J. C. Loder's lectures in osteology. Not only did he absorb a new discipline with amazing speed, but he began to oppose Loder's neat divisions and stratifications of living matter in the same way in which he had become skeptical of Linnaeus' great binomial organization of the vegetative kingdom. In search of a single, overall structural unity among vertebrates, he triumphantly claimed in 1784 to have found—correctly, as it turned out much later—the *os intermaxillare* in the human skull, a small bone in the upper jaw, extremely hard to identify, which according to contemporary professional anatomists was present in vertebrate animals but absent in human beings. It became truly a bone of contention and its absence came to be considered a human characteristic. Goethe was disheartened when he failed to receive any important support for his assertions. He did not publish his account of the intermaxillary bone until 1820, but by then his view had become more or less the accepted one.

By 1785, Goethe began to immerse himself in the study of plant life. As had been the case with his anatomical work, he showed little interest in detailed analysis unless it would stimulate or steer him toward the discovery of general laws of nature. However, once such a general principle came into view, he spared no effort in giving minute attention to those details which appeared to him to exemplify or illuminate them.

The formal and spiritual axis of Goethe's *Metamorphosis of Plants*, published in 1790,[2] is the *Urpflanze*, the prototypal plant, a vision of a dynamic pattern rather than the observation of any particular botanical specimen. The pattern he envisioned is "all leafiness," containing the potential for development into all of its organically interconnected parts.

Goethe divided the growth processes in dicotyledenous plants—and he restricted himself to them—into regular, irregular, and accidental. This last is meant to indicate atypical, or even monstrous, changes effected by insects or other external influences. Goethe proposed to deal only with "regular" (or "progressive") and "irregular" (or "regressive") metamorphosis. Progressive metamorphosis proceeds step by step from the first seed leaves to the final shaping of the fruit, and ascends by transformation—as though on a spiritual ladder—to the "pinnacle of nature": propagation by means of two sexes (Par. 6).

While progressive metamorphosis proceeds with "irresistible drive" and vigorous effort, in regressive metamorphosis these forces slacken and "leave their creature in an indecisive, soft condition which, though pleasurable to the eye, is inwardly unforceful and ineffective" (Par. 7). Growth, as a progressive development, proceeds from node to stem to leaf, and its typical transformations move from the yet unformed seed leaves to the more closely differentiated leaves, whereas the instruments of procreation are formed by a regression from the leaf which in turn signals the higher levels of development embodied by the various parts of the flower.

It is important to note how these two modes of transformation—progression and regression—differ in their manifestation. The stages of progressive development up to the moment of flowering are *successive,* while the sepals, petals, stamens, and pistil of the flower develop *simultaneously* (Par. 113). Goethe found that one can, in fact, force a plant into continual growth by bringing about an increased influx of its "cruder saps"; or, one can accelerate the advent of the flowering stage by withholding nutrients, thus causing a drawing together of the parts of the plant, so that all its organs are brought into a state of concentration and contiguity. Growth and flowering can therefore be seen as an alternation between expansion and concentration. "The same organ," Goethe wrote, "which was attached to the stem, expanded into a leaf and took on a highly differentiated form, now draws together in the calix, expands again as a petal, contracts into the sexual organs before expanding for the last time into the fruit," and in summarizing his new insight: ". . . a stamen is a contracted petal, just as we can say of the petal that it is a stamen in a state of expansion; a sepal is a leaf approaching a certain degree of purification, just as we can

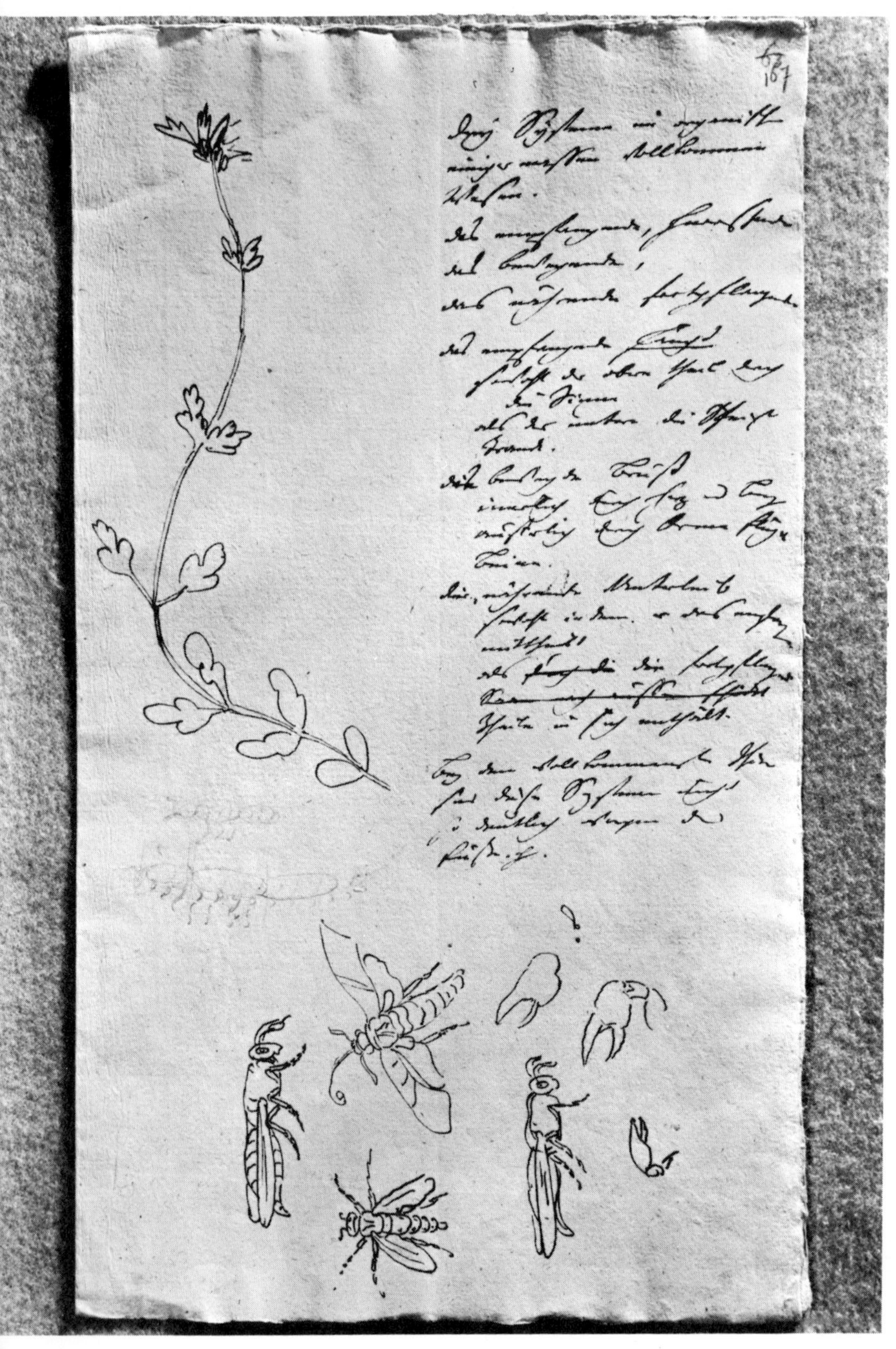

Morphological sketch and comment in Goethe's hand.
The text deals with animal typology.

say of the leaf that it is a sepal expanded as the result of the influx of cruder saps" (Par. 120). The development from seed leaves to flower in a typical dicotyledenous plant is upward, physically as well as spiritually.

The growth of the flower takes place as an interplay between opposing forces—the "vertical tendency" and the "spiral tendency." The former is that force which urges the plant in a "straight line toward the heavens"; the latter is the nourishing, multiplying principle which gives solidity to the plant. Only when both tendencies are in a dynamic balance, and in harmony with the general environment, can the plant develop normally without becoming a monstrosity. In concluding his late essay *Spiraltendenz der Vegetation,* Goethe associated these opposing tendencies with the male and female principle:

> . . . if we now see how the vertical tendency proves itself to be decisively masculine and the spiral tendency decisively feminine: then we can view all vegetation from the root up as though in secret and androgynous union; whereupon, as a consequence of the transformations inherent in growth, the two systems separate in clear contrast and juxtaposition, only to be united again in a higher sense.[3]

All vegetative growth and propagation takes place under the influences of polarity, metamorphosis, and heightening. The latter becomes even clearer when we see the spiritual quality with which Goethe imbues the flowering stage of his ideal plant, the result of the influx of a "purer liquid," (Par. 39) of the "finest filtration" (Par. 39) and "spiritual forces" (Par. 113). He believed that "purer airs" participated in the formation of the fruit. Moreover, all three of the basic forces come into play in a rhythmic pulse alternating between expansion and contraction, dissolution and concentration, systole and diastole.

NOTES

[1]*Physiognomische Fragmente zur Beförderung der Menschenkenntnis und Menschenliebe* (Leipzig and Winterthur, 1775–78).

[2]*Versuch die Metamorphose der Pflanzen zu erklären.* References to Goethe's essay are by paragraphs.

[3]*Hamb. Ausg.* XIII, p. 148.

3 • *Color Theory*

Although we find among Goethe's papers jottings concerning light and color as early as 1777, it was not until after his Italian journey in 1787 that he began a systematic inquiry. The final result was the publication in 1810 of two volumes entitled *Zur Farbenlehre*. The first contained the theory proper; the second, an extensive history of color theory, which has become a landmark in the historiography of science.[1]

The *locus classicus* of Goethe's theory is in the first part entitled *Didaktischer Theil*, containing an exposition of the theory. Contrary to *Metamorphosis of Plants*, Goethe was eminently conscious of colliding with the guild and with what was considered scientifically acceptable. His tone is more insistent throughout, and in the first volume an entire part is entitled *Polemischer Theil*. But even in the didactic section one can find an anti-mathematical and anti-Newtonian bias in such methodological considerations as the following:

> We do not set up arbitrary signs, letters, or whatever else might come to mind in place of the phenomena; here we do not take over outworn clichés which may be repeated a hundred times without thinking or even inducing thought in others, but rather, we are dealing with phe-

nomena which must exist concretely before the eyes of our body and our spirit, in order to develop with clarity (for ourselves and for others) their origin and derivation. [Par. 242]

This statement coincides with Goethe's repeated testy remark that Newton's color theory could have been written by and for a blind person.

The ultimate phenomena behind all colors are "darkness" and "light." They are not susceptible to further analysis and are regarded simply as *Urphänomene*, basic forces governing the universe. Since for Goethe reality is a result of the interaction between subject and object, it would be impossible for him to hold with Newton either that white is the sum of all colors or that black is the absence of color. Rather, darkness and light are cosmic principles which are the necessary conditions for color. In other words, colors result from the mingling of darkness and light. The basic colors are yellow and blue. Yellow results from seeing white through a medium of cloudiness or slight opacity; blue results from seeing darkness through a luminous medium. Hence, yellow is primarily related to light, blue to darkness. A perfectly balanced mixture of pure blue and pure yellow results in the color green. When the opacity through which white thickens increases, the yellow is intensified to orange (yellow plus red). Conversely, if the luminous medium through which one sees darkness becomes more transparent, then the blue is intensified to violet (blue plus red). The perfect combination of orange and violet results in the most majestic phenomenon in the hierarchy of colors: red. In this fashion Goethe completes a harmonious circle of colors:

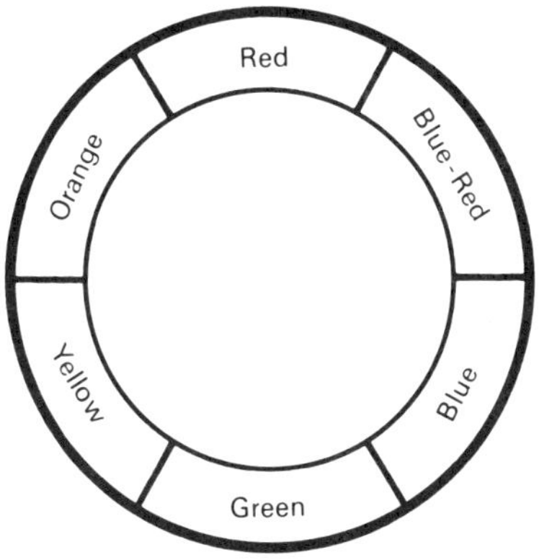

See Farbenlehre, par. 707

Elsewhere in the book, Goethe represents the same continuity of color as a doubling or overlapping of two triangles:

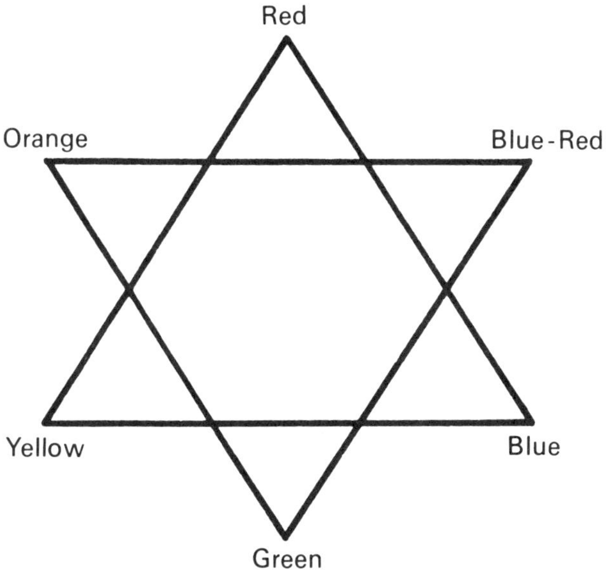

See Farbenlehre, par. 918

It is important to note that Goethe's harmonious circle does not include white, the particular bone of contention between himself and Newton. White is implicit in the circle as "light," in the same manner that black is implicit as "darkness." While whiteness is not equated to light, it approaches it:

> Everything living strives toward color, distinctness, specification, effect, opaqueness, and infinitely refined detail. Everything moribund is drawn toward whiteness, abstraction, generality, transfiguration, transparency. [Par. 586]

Pure space would appear to be perfectly transparent and "abstract," and the influx of matter into space is tantamount to an incursion of "opacity" *(das Trübe)*. Goethe stipulates an ideal light which is absolutely transparent and, hence, absolutely colorless. The color white is the phenomenon nearest absolute transparency and therefore the most refined, most nearly abstract color:

> Pure translucent dimness stems from transparency. . . . [Par. 146]
> The perfection of dimness is White, the most indifferent, brightest, first, non-transparent occupancy of space. [Par. 147]

Neither the circle nor the hexagon is intended by Goethe to represent a fixed system. All colors constantly shift and oscillate, attaining purity only in ideal and ephemeral moments. Each color in the orbit around the circle can be seen either as a result of the darkening of its nearest "higher" neighbor or as a lightening of its "lower" one. Because of our physiological responses, Goethe calls one side (the one moving up from yellow) the "plus side," and the other (moving up from blue) the "minus side." Countenancing yellow and orange makes us "agile, lively, ambitious," while blue and violet evokes "uneasiness, languidness, and yearning."[2]

The circle is a natural result of an "activity" which relates the observer to the phenomenon of color:

> By nature the eye demands totality and completes a color circle of its own. In violet, which is demanded by yellow, are contained red and blue; in orange, which corresponds to blue, are contained yellow and the red; green unites the blue and yellow, and yellow demands red. . . . [Par. 60]

The overlapping triangles, even more than the circle, allows for a mystical interpretation:

> Finally it may be surmised that color is susceptible to a mystical interpretation. For inasmuch as that scheme in which the multifariousness of colors may be represented alludes to archetypal relationships which belong to human vision *(Anschauung)* as well as to nature, there can hardly be any doubt that one can avail oneself of these relationships, as it were, as a language, even when one wishes to express those archetypal relationships which do not impinge on the senses with such great force. The mathematician has great esteem for the value and usefulness of the triangle; the triangle has a position of high honor among the mystics; a good many phenomena can be schematized by the triangle, such as the phenomenon of color, in such a manner that by means of doubling and overlapping one arrives at the ancient and mysterious hexagon. [Par. 918]

R. D. Gray has shown that the essence of Goethe's color theory goes back to the poet's early passionate preoccupation with alchemy and mysticism.[3] Goethe was conversant with the seventeenth-century mystic Jacob Böhme. He had studied the *Aura Catena Homeri* of the early eighteenth century, its cryptic symbols and baroque doctrine of opposing universal elements and its venerable analogies between the microcosm of man and the macrocosm of nature. He was familiar, as Goethe put it, with "mystic cabbalistic chemistry."[4] One must acknowledge these roots.

At the same time it is well to realize that neither the *Morphology* nor the *Theory of Color* are written in the vein of mystical tracts. Goethe himself, learned as he was in mystical works of the Renaissance,[5] had a low opinion of their suitability for natural science. He was careful at the end of the *Theory of Color* to emphasize that the circle or hexagon are not mystical in themselves, but "lend themselves to allegoric, symbolic, or mystic interpretation." He distinguished between the three, and cut short such excursions into mysticism in order not to expose himself to the charge of engaging in "rhapsodic ramblings" (*Schwärmerei*).

Moreover, we read among his aphoristic pronouncements: "[Alchemy] is the misuse of what is genuine and true, a leap from the idea, from the possible to the real, a false employment of genuine feelings, a deceitful promise, whereby our dearest hopes and wishes are flattered."[6] Goethe was a meticulous experimenter, and the accounts of his experiments are flawless. Only inasmuch as he opposed explanations of natural phenomena by means of causal sequences and was interested in a discipline that is not based on mathematics,[7] must we recognize that Goethe was not a "scientist" in the modern sense. Rather, he was a pilgrim through nature, who with poetic imagination and a majestic, creative consciousness arrived at insights which encompassed both value and fact. In that sense, his work represents a miraculous reconstruction of harmonious human sensibilities which had long before been divided and alienated from each other. Poetry and science were united in Goethe's mind as two modes of interpreting and expressing a heightened human consciousness. Once one comes to see that he could not accept the Cartesian geometrical world view, nor the Newtonian ideal detachment from natural processes, then it is not surprising that such seemingly disparate fields as morphology and color theory should be analogous in their basic premises and even in important details. This fact can readily be understood as the result of Goethe's insistence on personal involvement in the act of observation and interpretation. *Zarte Empirie* ("delicate empriricism") and insights are concomitants of intense spiritual activity and are always an interplay between observer and the observed. A human consciousness is as much a part of nature as is the life of a plant or the color of the moon seen through an evening mist.

Polar opposites in the form of "the masculine" and "the feminine" are *Urphänomene* in Goethe's morphology appearing either as the vertical or the horizontal principles and joining to produce the "spiral tendency," or else in their heightened forms as sexual organs which come into being to fulfill the plant's highest purpose. The principle of metamorphosis is implicit in the assumption of a basic leaf-like configuration *(Urpflanze)* from which all other parts of dicotyledenous plants are derived. Heightening *(Steigerung)* is the force behind metamorphosis of organisms because each successive form of the leaf is an advancement toward a goal—the flower—which is the ultimate intensification of a capacity inherent in the original configuration.

A similar analysis can be made of Gothe's circle or hexagon of colors: Light and Darkness are *Urphänomene* to which all colors are related. With blue and yellow stipulated as basic colors, all other shades are seen as a progression toward or regression from them, at varying levels of metamorphosis. Colors are not neutral or indifferent in value, but tend towards the dignity and majesty of red to which Goethe assigns the special name *Purpur*, alluding to the fact that it is preeminently a regal color. Its position at the top of the circle and hexagon has both conceptual and symbolical significance.

But beyond these general analogies there are also more specific similarities. As the "highest" color, red results from an increase in darkness (heightening of either orange or violet), so the flowering stage in the plant is ushered in by a "contraction of the leaves from their periphery" (Par. 29) and by their assembly "around a single point" (Par. 33, 116); a concentration and increase in density (or darkness) take place before the plant reaches its highest stage. Moreover, this stage is induced by a reduction of the growth processes and in that sense constitutes a turning inward and thereby a final realization of its own potential.

Perhaps most important of all is the remarkable congruence of the progress of time in the formation of the flower and in the final movement toward red in Goethe's circle of color. The flower appears to arise during the briefest possible moment approaching the zero point, inasmuch as all parts contributing to the flower develop simultaneously rather than successively. The flowering process is therefore a moment of spatial and temporal concentration containing within it the ultimate distillation of all previous stages experienced in well-defined segments of time and within the context of various physical forms.

In his *Theory of Color*, Goethe points to the ephemeral quality of all colors and the difficulties of determining a precise blue or a precise yellow. An even greater instability applies to the color red, which he calls "the culmination point." Here, as in the flowering stage of the plant, a point of infinitely compressed infinity has been reached, and here as in the plant, the "culminating" moment contains the distillate of past experience. While red is associated with the "highest" visible manifestation of life, this color is also in the immediate vicinity of non-being and death. In the circle it is the most unstable of all colors, and at the same time a dynamic integration of all other colors: "Whoever knows how red arises prismatically will not consider it paradoxical when we assert that this color contains, partly *actu* partly *potentia*, all other colors" (Par. 793).

Because floral color is a manifestation of life, it is, no matter how beautiful, imperfect and impure. The "highest" color, resulting from completely purified saps, would not be red but white: "The appearance of beautiful colors leads us to the thought that the material which fills the petals has attained a high degree of purity, but not yet the highest where it appears to us as white and without color" (*Metamorphosis of Plants*, par. 45).

In *Metamorphosis of Plants*, the idea of white as a manifestation of floral perfection appears like a sudden intrusion from another realm. The essay does not prepare the reader to expect any particular color for the flower or even for the *Urpflanze*. The symbolical significance of white, therefore, can be fathomed only after Goethe's color theory has been thoroughly absorbed. It seems to me that the reiteration of an idea which in one instance (in *Metamorphosis*) appears out of keeping with the essay, provides particularly strong evidence that Goethe's yearning toward the unity of all nature—toward a unified vision of it—was overwhelming. One might, in fact, look at other of Goethe's scientific endeavors, for instance in geology or meteorology, and find important analogies, though probably nowhere in as decisive a cluster as in the two areas discussed here.

Conclusive evidence exists that Goethe intended to compose a large "nature poem," under the inspiration of his close friend Knebel who had sent him his translation of Lucretius' *De Rerum Natura*. Goethe completed no more than a fragment, in hexameters, entitled "Metamorphose der Tiere," but to satisfy his abiding interest in a poetic rendition of his basic outlook on nature, he placed it with a group of other nature poems. Thus in the 1827 edition of Goethe's collected works, under the heading "Gott und Welt," there are in addition to "Metamorphose der Tiere" such poems as "Metamorphose der Pflanzen," "Dauer im Wechsel," and "Eins und Alles," in which scientific ideas are made lyrically visible. Goethe apparently never quite abandoned the hope of arriving at an all-embracing outlook which would tie together all fields of knowledge. In a letter to a friend written in 1810, he directed himself—in a manner conjuring up the Pythagorean tradition—to the problem of finding the basic laws underlying tonal sequences and musical composition:

> Zelter is now here and probably his presence will promote my wish to make my own views applicable also to the theory of harmony, so that the latter may be tied directly to all physical phenomena and also to the *Theory of Color*. If a few great formulas can be worked out

successfully, then everything will be as One, unfold from One, and return to One.[8]

In many of Goethe's prose passages, and indeed in some of his poetry, the borderline between science and poetry is vague, a fact which need not reduce the value of his nature poems as poetry, nor undermine the insights expressed in the form and pace of "scientific" prose. Poetry shines through even when Goethe reports on his observation of the smallest and most circumscribed physical details, such as the diameter of a beaver's tibia and fibula,[9] minutiae which appear poetic in Goethe because they have become "visible ideas," variants of a presumed archetypal *Gestalt* and parts of a living cosmic organization.

Natural phenomena in Goethe's world are both factually and symbolically true, and in articulating their symbolic meanings it is easy to see how Goethe's language glides easily into what one would call poetry. Here, for example, is a discursive passage arbitrarily chosen from a section entitled *Licht und Finsternis zum Auge:*

> When wir die Augen innerhalb eines ganz finsteren Raums offen halten, so wird uns ein gewisser Mangel empfindbar. Das Organ ist sich selbst überlassen, es zieht sich in sich selbst zurück, ihm fehlt jene reizende befriedigende Berührung, durch die es mit der äusseren Welt verbunden und zum Ganzen wird. [*Farbenlehre,* par. 6]

> If we keep our eyes open in a completely darkened room, we become aware of a certain deficiency. The organ is left to itself; it withdraws into itself and lacks that stimulating and satisfying contact by which it becomes whole and united to the external world.

Conversely, Goethe can make the data received through

close and detailed "scientific" observation an integral part of a poem:

> Werdend betrachte sie nun, wie nach und nach sich die Pflanze,
>   Stufenweise geführt, bildet zu Blüten und Frucht.
> Aus dem Samen entwickelt sie sich, sobald ihn der Erde
> Stille befruchtender Schoss hold in das Leben entlässt,
> Und dem Reize des Lichts, des heiligen, ewig bewegten,
> Gleich den zärtesten Bau keimender Blätter empfiehlt.[10]

> Now see it develop, how by and by the plant is
> guided in stages, and fashions its blossoms and fruit.
> It arises, as soon as the quietly fertile
> earth-womb releases the seed into life
> and commends to the charm of the light, eternally
>   changing and sacred,
> the tenderest structure of budding leaves.

NOTES

[1]In addition, there is a third slimmer volume containing only illustrations. References to Goethe's *Theory of Color* are by paragraphs.

[2]*Farbenlehre*, par. 764, 777.

[3]*Goethe the Alchemist* (Cambridge, 1952).

[4]. . . am meisten aber verbarg ich vor Herder meine mystischkabbalistische Chemie und was sich auf sie bezog." *(Dichtung und Wahrheit* II, p. 10.)

[5]See Harold Jantz, *Goethe the Renaissance Man* (Princeton, 1951).

[6]*Jubiläums.* XL, p. 180.

[7]"Dass eine Physik unabhängig von der Mathematik existiere, davon schien man keinen Begriff mehr zu haben." *(Hamb. Ausg.* XIV, p. 265.)

[8]Letter to Sartorius, July 19, 1810.

[9]*Hamb. Ausg.* XIII, p. 209.

[10]From the poem "Metamorphose der Pflanzen," *Hamb. Ausg.* I, p. 199.

II · MORPHOLOGY AND *FAUST*

1 • General Outlook

It is not surprising that Goethe found a niche in *Faust* for some of his most dearly held views on the nature of the physical world, particularly in the second part of the poem, all of which was written after he had turned fifty. Probably the best known "scientific" passages in *Faust* are those speculations in Part II about the forming of the earth's surface either by a series of catastrophic events such as earthquakes and volcanic eruptions ("Vulcanism"), or else by oceanic sediments and erosion ("Neptunism"). In the "Classical Walpurgis Night," Anaxagoras and Thales engage in a debate over the merits of their respective world views:

ANAXAGORAS:
> Hast du, O Thales, je in einer Nacht
> Solch einen Berg aus Schlamm hervorgebracht?

THALES:
> Nie war Natur und ihr lebendiges Fliessen
> Auf Tag und Nacht und Stunden angewiesen.
> Sie bildet regelnd jegliche Gestalt,
> Und selbst im Grossen ist es nicht Gewalt.

ANAXAGORAS:
> Hier aber war's! Plutonisch grimmig Feuer,
> Äolischer Dünste Knallkraft, ungeheuer,

Durchbrach des flachen Bodens alte Kruste,
Dass neu sogleich ein Berg entstehen musste.

[7859–68]

ANAXAGORAS
  Have you, O Thales, made at any time
  Within one night a mountain out of slime?
THALES
  Never was Nature, with her fluid powers,
  Reduced to scale of days or nights or hours.
  Thus every form by law she will create;
  No violence she uses to be great.
ANAXAGORAS
  But here she did! Plutonic, searing fire,
  Aeolian gusts, with thundrous vapours dire,
  Racked the old crust of level earth, broke through,
  And thus a new born mountain rose to view.[1]

Somewhat less explicit from a scientific point of view is the light symbolism in the first scene of Part II where Faust awakens to the majestic spectacle of the rising sun to which he brashly turns, yearning to receive fulfillment of his "highest wish." Unable to stand up to the "sea of flames," he must turn away and be content with the reflected radiance of a rainbow. This is not to be interpreted as the Platonic pale reflection of an idea, but more properly as a differentation by color and form of an archetypal phenomenon. The pure light of the sun is not compatible with human life. It is undifferentiated, beyond perception, and accessible only through mirror images, allegory, and symbolization:

Sie tritt hervor!—und leider schon geblendet,
Kehr ich mich weg, vom Augenschmerz durchdrungen
. . . .
So bleibe denn die Sonne mir im Rücken!

Der Wassersturz, das Felsenriff durchbrausend,
Ihn schau' ich an mit wachsendem Entzückcn.

. . . .

Allein wie herrlich, diesem Sturm erspriessend,
Wölbt sich des bunten Bogens Wechseldauer,
Bald rein gezeichnet, bald in Luft zerfliessend,
Umher verbreitend duften kühle Schauer.
D e r spiegelt ab das menschliche Bestreben.
Ihm sinne nach, und du begreifst genau:
Im farbigen Abglanz haben wir das Leben.

[4701–27]

The dazzling sun strides forth, and fills the air.
I turn, from greater power than eyes can bear.

. . . .

And so I turn, the sun upon my shoulders,
To watch the waterfall, with heart elate,
The cataract pouring, crashing from the boulders,

. . . .
And then how splendid
To see the rainbow rising from this rage,
Now clear, now dimmed, in cool sweet vapour blended.
So strive the figures on our mortal stage.
This ponder well, the mystery closer seeing;
In mirrored hues we have our life and being.

These magnificent lines show a paradoxical moment of resignation and ecstasy, in which the restraints of aesthetic form serve not only as a reminder of our human condition, but also as inducements to the highest inward activity and delight. In any case, the unique word *Wechseldauer* (1. 4722), coined by Goethe to characterize the rainbow, could be applied to the circle of color whose permanence consists in an everlasting orbital progression of transitions.

I do not believe that it is profitable for our purpose to point to additional scientific positions or theories as they may appear in the context of *Faust*.[2] Instead, the attempt to arrive at an overall structural view will yield results of greater aesthetic relevance. Such an attempt calls for efforts akin to what in natural science Goethe may have meant by "activity." He had noted, we remember, that only activity could unite theory and experience and that the attempt to fuse these irreconcilable polarities by logic and reflection could produce only cerebral phantoms and illusions (see p. 16).

But a poem, while consisting of words is, in a Goethean sense, also a natural organism; the reader of poetry must therefore call upon the same inward powers as the scientist. Like the plant to the biologist, the poem is a "self-revealing mystery" to the reader. One must guard against the danger of proliferating and poorly supported analogies. But the risk is acceptable, it seems to me, in view of the unusually exciting prospect before us: a body of concepts and images which support and inform two almost lifelong preoccupations of Goethe—his *Faust* poem and his efforts in the natural sciences.

NOTES

[1]Goethe, *Faust, Part Two,* tr. Philip Wayne (Baltimore, 1959). For all quotations from *Faust II,* I used Philip Wayne's translation, with the exception of some lines on pp. 95, 117, and 131, as noted.

[2]Wilhelm Emrich (op. cit., p. 141) points to a gardener's song in *Faust II* which in his view refers to the "simultaneity" in the development of the parts of a single flower:

> Unter lustigen Gewinden,
> In geschmückter Lauben Bucht,
> Alles ist zugleich zu finden:
> Knospe, Blätter, Blume, Frucht.

[5174–77]

This interpretation is not tenable since the fruit does not develop simultaneously with the death of the blossom but after it. The gardener is here simply referring to his own activity of bringing together different decorative plants at various stages of development.

2 · *Polarity*

A review of the progressive stages in the genesis of Goethe's drama from *Urfaust* (circa 1773) to the completion of *Faust II* in 1831 could easily obscure the structure of the finished work as we know it. In this connection it may be sufficient to point out that the idea of polarity, while implicit in the *Urfaust* (as it was in *Werther*) was then still very much in the background and had probably not reached the level of conscious working principle with Goethe. From *Werther* one receives the impact of the fatal tension between *Einschränkung* und *Entgrenzung*, between the straightjacket of human and social limitations, and the thrust toward an emotional absolute, the untainted and the divine. One can say that Werther is a truly tragic hero—and as such almost unique among Goethe's major characters—whose fatal flaw and "sickness onto death," his emotional absolutism, is also the condition of his greatness. Any compromise between the two opposing forces in his make-up would be at odds with his nature. In its inexorable and accelerating thrust toward catastrophe, *Werther* is in the tradition of *Oedipus Rex*.

There is an analogy between the polar dualities inherent in the characters of Werther and Faust. Like Werther's,

Faust's despair stems from the conflict between the narrow confines of his human condition and an awareness of the cosmic totality and truth lying forever beyond his grasp. But Faust is a heightened Werther, in the sense that his despair not only comes from emotional and sensual frustrations, but that it encompasses the entire range of human incapacities—physical, intellectual, emotional, metaphysical:

FAUST:
> Nur mit Entsetzen wach' ich morgens auf,
> Ich möchte bittre Tränen weinen,
> Den Tag zu sehn, der mir in seinem Lauf
> Nicht E i n e n Wunsch erfüllen wird, nicht E i n e n,
> Der selbst die Ahnung jeder Lust
> Mit eigensinnigem Krittel mindert,
> Die Schöpfung meiner regen Brust
> Mit tausend Lebensfratzen hindert.

[1554–61]

FAUST:
> I awake with horror in the morning,
> and bitter tears well up in me
> when I must face each day that in its course
> cannot fulfill a single wish, not one!
> The very intimations of delight
> are shattered by the carpings of the day
> which foil the inventions of my eager soul
> with a thousand leering grimaces of life.

Faust *begins* in despair but has the capacity to transcend the impulse to suicide, whereas Werther's irreversible path *ends* in self-destruction. Faust sets out on his dynamic quest at a point where Werther had suffered his shipwreck, and in comparison to Werther, Faust's travail yields levels of self-awareness for which Werther lacked the native capacity. Such awareness is crucial and becomes even more profound as Goethe moves toward the completion of the first part of the drama. In these lines in *Faust I,* which were still absent in the *Urfaust* and in the fragment of 1790, Faust says:

> Du bist dir nur des einen Triebs bewusst;
> O lerne nie den anderen kennen!
> Zwei Seelen wohnen, ach! in meiner Brust,
> Die eine will sich von der anderen trennen;
>
> [1110–13]

> You only know a single passion;
> O do not try to know the other!
> Two souls, alas, dwell in my breast,
> each seeks to sever from the other.

The "two souls" can be grouped with other articulations of Faust's dilemma. They are reflections of the eternal conflict between the relative and the absolute, the limited and the infinite.

There is also the polar opposition between Mephisto and Faust. It too received increasing articulation, complexity, and explicitly metaphysical dimension when Goethe resumed work on the drama in 1796. In the original version, Mephisto is still more closely patterned on the chapbook devil of the sixteenth century, and as such the evil, powerful purveyor of infernal magic. The Mephisto of the final version is less a character from folklore than an eschatological force, more the perennial negator and ironist than the personification of evil. He belongs to the divine order of things and the Lord addresses him without enmity in the "Prologue in Heaven":

Du darfst auch da nur frei erscheinen;
Ich habe deinesgleichen nie gehasst.

. . . .

Drum geb' ich ihm den Gesellen zu,
Der reizt und wirkt und muss als Teufel schaffen.—

[336–343]

I am glad to let you have apparent freedom;
I hold no hatred for the like of you.

. . . .

I'm therefore pleased to give him a companion
who must goad and prod and be a devil.—

While the unfolding of the fable depends heavily on those polar antitheses, there are clusters of lesser dualities which gather about many of the *Faust* scenes: feeling versus intellect, insight versus learning, intellect versus instinct, Nordic or Gothic gloom versus Mediterranean clarity, fertile humidity versus sterile dryness. The list could be greatly extended, perhaps along the lines of a note jotted down by Goethe under the heading of "Qualitäten":

> Wir und die Gegenstände,
> Licht und Finsternis,
> Leib und Seele,
> Geist und Materie,
> Gott und die Welt,
> Gedanke und Ausdehnung,
> Ideales und Reales,
> Sinnlichkeit und Vernunft,
> Phanatasie und Verstand,
> Sein und Sehnsucht.[1]

> Ourselves and the objects,
> Light and darkness,

> Body and soul,
> Spirit and matter,
> Thought and extension,
> Ideal and real,
> Sensuousness and intellect,
> Imagination and reason,
> Being and yearning.

But at least equally interesting are the less obvious, though no less pervasive, dualities playing out their confrontations in the style of the mature and aged Goethe. It is a kind of poetic word game, which in a sense repeats the progress of the "two souls" in Faust's breast, and that of other explicit pairs of opposites as well. The chief game is the game of poetry itself which exists as a highly conscious activity. It not only records and reflects the progress of dramatic action, but also plays, as it were, with its own mode of existence. We know from frequent statements made by Goethe that for him poetry was a realm of spiritual activity in which abstract concepts and concrete events could be fused into the "visible idea," or in modern terms, into the Concrete Universal. The poetry in *Faust* does not rest within itself, but in crucial moments sportingly struggles for its justification and existence. The game is carried out most conspicuously between Faust and Mephistopheles; but frequently the poetry has a way of turning upon itself without attaching itself to one or the other of the cast of characters. The general effect of this activity, this *ludus humanus* played out between consciousness and the objects of its purvey, is one of irony hovering between affirmation and denial of every image or proposition.

The ironic mode begins simply enough with satirical attacks on conventions and institutions, as when Mephisto, by means of mock-serious admonitions to a new student, ridicules the pretensions of academic disciplines. In another scene, Mephisto imitates the unctuous voice of a parson, thereby satirizing the church and its less savory representatives:

> Die Kirch' allein, meine lieben Frauen,
> Kann ungerechtes Gut verdauen.
>
> [2839–2840]

> The church alone, dear women, can digest
> ill-gotten gains without a stomach ache.

When Faust's encounter with Gretchen stirs in him tenderness and love, Mephisto ironically demeans such love into crass sexuality:

> Gut und schön!
> Dann wird von ewiger Treu' und Liebe,
> Von einzig überallmächt'gem Triebe—
> Wird das auch so von Herzen gehn?
>
> [3055–58]

> That's good of you!
> And then you'll speak of faith and love eternal,
> of a single, overpowering urge—
> will that flow as easily from your heart?

In the interview early in the drama with his famulus, Faust responds to Wagner's shallow optimism concerning human perfectibility "Und wie wir's dann zuletzt so herrlich weit gebracht" ("how very far we've come today") with the cynical answer "O ja, bis an die Sterne weit!" ("O, yes, a journey to the heavens!") [572–73]

There are many such examples in *Faust I.* The irony is direct and expresses the tension between what is said and what is meant. There is hardly an oscillation between the two poles; the entire weight falls on what is meant. Such utterances are transparent, and by ironically expressing approval, the attack on the intended victim, be it the church, the academy, eros, or faith in human progress, is given a keen cutting edge. In *Dichtung und Wahrheit*, Goethe described such irony as it was used by the contemporary essayist Gottlieb Wilhelm Rabener. Clearly, at this point, Goethe no longer held such a stylistic mode in high esteem:

> . . . but Rabener makes too much use of direct irony in that he praises the blameworthy and blames the praiseworthy; . . . this rhetorical device should be used only on the rarest occasions; for in the long run it will bore intelligent men, confuse the weak, though true enough, it will give pleasure and comfort to a large middle class which may think of itself—without any special intellectual effort—as more clever than others.[2]

That kind of satire, almost entirely absent in Goethe's mature poetry, is largely confined to such polemical writings as the *Xenien* in the late 1790s. However, in addition to direct satire, the ironic mode made its appearance in the Frankfurt years during the early 1770s. How deeply Goethe was steeped in this form when he began work on *Faust* may be seen in several fragments he sketched and then laid aside. This passage from *Der Ewige Jude* (1774) offers a good example of a provocatively flippant style used for the treatment of a lofty subject:

> Der Vater sass auf seinem Thron,
> Da rief er seinen lieben Sohn,
> (Der Vater war ganz aufgebracht

Und sprach: Das hast du dumm gemacht,
Sieh einmal auf die Erde)
Musst' zwei bis drei mal schreien.
Da kam der Sohn ganz überquer,
Gestolpert über Sterne her
Und fragt', was zu befehlen.[3]

The Father sat upon his throne
and called to his beloved Son,
(The Father was a bit upset
and said: You didn't do things properly;
just take a look at earth below)
two times or three he had to shout.
Then stumbling over stars and planets
the son traversed to meet his Father
and asked him: what commandest Thou?

These bumptious verses make God and Christ inaccessible to direct emotional or intellectual apprehension. Being a facetious imitation of a puppet-theater treatment of such subjects, they constitute a kind of twice-removed parody. Such playfulness is not arrogant, but rather a complicated form of humility that stems from a reluctance to refer to the deity directly.[4] This ironic style proved to be a more penetrating poetic vehicle than satire, and examples of it can be found throughout the *Faust* poem. Its basic characteristic is an incongruity between manner and matter, as when solemn and profound thoughts are expressed in casual, even irreverent language. The opening monologue of Faust's despondency is a modified doggerel verse, a form strongly reminiscent of sixteenth century *Knittelvers* once practiced by the most famous *Meistersinger*, Hans Sachs.

Another composition in a doggerel-type verse, *Hanswursts Hochzeit* (*Pickelherring's Wedding*), with the

explicatory subtitle "A Microcosmic Drama," is replete
with earthy references to the human anatomy and comes
with an enormous list of characters whose names are
sufficiently outrageous to preempt for themselves a major
part of the play's meager dramatic substance. The first
few lines of this little work rather surprisingly have the
feeling-tone and even the syntactical make-up of the
opening monologue of *Faust*. A character named Kilian
Brustfleck opens the play with this lament:

> Hab' ich endlich mit vielem Fleiss,
> Manchen moralisch politischem Schweiss
> Meinen Mündel Hanswurst erzogen
> Und ihn ziemlich zurechtgebogen
>
> . . . .
>
> Seine Lust in den Weg zu . . . ,
> Hab' nicht können aus der Wurzel reissen.[5]

> After expending much work and trouble
> and streams of moral-political sweat
> to educate my charge *Hanswurst*
> and twist him into proper shape
>
> . . . .
>
> I have not been able to uproot
> his desire to shit on the trail.

The cadence of these lines is not far removed from
that of the opening monologue of the *Urfaust*.

> Hab nun, ach, die Philosophey,
> Medizin und Juristerey,
> Und leider auch Theologie
> Durchaus studiert mit heisser Müh.
> Da steh ich nun, ich armer Tor,
> Und bin so klug als wie zuvor.[6]

> Alas I've studied philosophy,
> medicine and jurisprudence
> and to my sorrow theology;
> studied them well with ardent zeal.
> Yet here I am a wretched fool,
> no wiser than I was before.

Faust's complaint, almost as blunt as Kilian Brustfleck's, is written in "bad verse" according to the standards of the eighteenth century. An audience of children is not expected to reflect on this, but an adult observer will be like a parent who stands aside in order to watch a multiple spectacle: one performed by the puppets, the other by his entranced children, and perhaps a third by a puppeteer manipulating his figures and impersonating with his voice the various stock characters; that is to say, the opening lines of the *Faust* drama are fragmented into at least three levels. Nor are they at all simple—as their tone ironically leads one to believe—but involved, sophisticated, and problematic. The possibility of a turn to high seriousness is always present, a potential that is periodically realized. Thus after less than forty lines of monologue, the syllabic accents become regular, the tone unironic and unambiguous. Manner and matter are harmoniously united:

> Ach! könnt' ich nur auf Bergeshöhn
> In deinem lieben Lichte gehn,
> Um Bergeshöhle mit Geistern schweben,
> Auf Wiesen in deinem Dämmer weben,
> Von allem Wissensqualm entladen,
> In deinem Tau gesund mich baden!
>
> [392–97]

> If I could roam on mountain heights in
> your dear light,

> drift with hovering spirits over caverns,
> weave over meadows in your twilight glow,
> I would expel the smoke of learning
> and be drenched to wholeness in your dew.

This irony is sustained by Faust until the growling poodle in his study reveals himself as Mephistopheles (l. 1323ff.). Faust's elaborate magical evocation of the four elemental spirits is climaxed by a final imperious brandishing of the crucifix. Only then is Mephisto forced out of his poodle's disguise. Yet this strident transformation evokes from the newly emerged Mephistopheles no more than a dispassionate reference to physiological responses: "Ihr habt mich weidlich schwitzen machen" ("I've sweated thoroughly for you") (l. 1325). Mephistopheles is the agent of disillusionment; he does all he can to prevent a reconciliation of opposites. As the emperor of numbers and facts he wishes to extend his rule over all creation. As early as in the "Prologue in Heaven" he reveals himself as the no-nonsense rationalist bent on breaking down the artifacts of poetry into their prosaic constituents. The "Spirit that denies" extends his corrosive influence even into the verbal environment which he inhabits. His target, along with Faust's soul, is the poetic imagination which meaningfully and miraculously binds together the phenomena of life.

> Vom Kribskrabs der Imagination
> Hab' ich dich doch auf Zeiten lang kuriert;
> [3268–70]

> I think I cured you for some time to come
> from the claptrap of your fantasy;

Earlier in the play, when Faust had resolved to encompass all the world's suffering and all its joys within the confines of his own soul, his antagonist answers:

> Assoziiert Euch mit einem Poeten,
> Lasst den Herrn in Gedanken schweifen,
> Und alle edlen Qualitäten
> Auf Euren Ehrenscheitel häufen,
> Des Löwen Mut,
> Des Hirsches Schnelligkeit,
> Des Italieners feurig Blut,
> Des Norden Dau'rbarkeit.

[1789–97]

> Make your alliance with a poet
> and let that gentleman think lofty thoughts,
> and let him heap the noblest qualities
> upon your worthy head:
> a lion's nerve,
> a stag's rapidity,
> the fiery blood of Italy,
> the constancy of northern man.

Clearly the "poet" in the context of these lines stands for one who conjures up empty illusions of the kind which Faust continuously creates for himself. Mephisto ridicules Faust's vast ambition and flippantly proposes that he make himself the subject of poetic imagination, because only in this way could he hope to fulfill his desires. In other words, he tells Faust in an insulting manner that he has lost contact with the sorry reality of his human existence. At the same time, however, one comes to realize that the images of Faust's fantasy are indeed the stuff of poetry, that Mephistopheles is merely describing the context of Faust's as well as of his own existence, which is imaginary and poetic. In fact, these deceptively simple lines contain a triumphant implication: the meaning and structure of "reality" is ultimately poetic and aesthetic; a chaotic world crystallizes into form and meaning only as it is screened and channeled through the "exact imagination" of the poet.

Near the end of the third act of *Faust II*, as the magic illusion of Helen of Troy's presence dissolves before us, there is an exchange between the chorus of handmaidens and Panthalis, their leader, who scolds her underlings for not joining their queen, Helena, in Hades. According to Panthalis, they will have no individual existence without the reflected glory of their mistress, Helena:

> Wer keinen Namen sich erwarb noch Edles will,
> Gehört den Elementen an; so fahret hin!
>
> [9981–82]

> Who no fair name has won, nor strives for noble things,
> Belongs, but to the elements: so get you gone!

Indeed they turn into trees, nymphs, vines, and naiads. Here the poet emerges as something more than a maker of poetry. For if the handmaidens have not earned a name for themselves, it is because poets have not found them worthy of glorification as individuals.

Faust is by no means the only composition in which Goethe dwells on the intimate relationship between hero and poet, and on the power of poetry to define and shape the shapeless, hovering shadows of passing humanity. In "Euphrosyne" (1797–98), the dying heroine exclaims:

> Lass nicht ungerühmt mich zu den Schatten hinabgehen!
> Nur die Muse gewährt einiges Leben dem Tod.
> Denn gestaltlos schweben umher in Persephoneias
> Reiche, massenweis, Schatten von Namen getrennt;

Wen der Dichter aber gerühmt, der wandelt, gestaltet,
Einzeln, gesellet dem Chor aller Heroen sich zu.
[121–26]

Let me not descend to the shadows un-praised!
  Only the muses may grant some life to the dead.
For floating shapeless in Persephone's regions,
  Are the teeming shadows bereft of their names;
But he whom the poet has praised walks apart
  And formed, and will join the choir of heroes.

The same thought is conveyed when the Princess admonishes her bewildered poet-friend Tasso:

Und schienst noch kurz vorher so rein zu fühlen,
Wie Held und Dichter für einander leben,
Wie Held und Dichter sich einander suchen
Und keiner je den Andern neiden soll?
Zwar herrlich ist die liedeswerte Tat,
Doch schön ist's auch, der Taten stärkste Fülle
Durch würd'ge Lieder auf die Nachwelt bringen.
[801–07]

And just before you seemed to feel so well
How hero and poet live for one another,
Seek one another, and how neither may
Envy the other. It is true that deeds
Worthy of song are splendid, but to bring
The fullness of such deeds, in worthy songs,
Down to posterity, is also fine.[7]

There is also subtle irony in a passage from *Iphigenie*, where Pylades reprimands his bosom friend Orestes for being too ambitious in demanding that all his deeds of the moment be the subject of future song and poetry:

Wir möchten jede Tat
So gross gleich tun, als wie sie wächst und wird,

Wenn jahrelang durch Länder und Geschlechter
Der Mund der Dichter sie vermehrend wälzt.
[682–85]

    We would every deed
At once perform as grandly as it shows
After long ages, when from land to land
The poet's swelling song hath roll'd it on.[8]

The hope that future generations may sing the glories of a hero is frequently voiced in Homer's *Odyssey*. The goddess Athena and the aged Nestor, the Gerenian horseman, put manly courage into the timid and childlike heart of Telemachus, Odysseus' son, and King Alcinous successfully pleads with Odysseus to recount his adventures before reaching the land of the Phaeacians.[9] By varying the phrase and the context, Goethe succeeds in severing the dramatic action of *Iphigenie* from its temporal restriction, for the public is well aware of the legendary fame of Orestes. Therefore, if Pylades speaks of Orestes as desiring such fame in a new dramatic context, it puts the reader into a reflective frame of mind which acts counter to his suspension of disbelief. And the hint that the reality of Orestes' existence is poetic rather than historical should not be missed. The polarities in this instance are permanence and universality on the one hand, historicity and concreteness on the other.

Mephisto's suggestion to Faust that he associate himself with a poet is irony of a similar sort. It is a stylistic mode which is characteristic of Goethe's mature manner, and constitutes a high point in a development which has a modest and rather conventional beginning. Its stages can be conveniently traced through the *Faust* poem itself, keeping in mind the fact that Goethe spent almost sixty years on its composition. By its nature, the "Prologue in Heaven" places Faust, the Man, *sub specie aeternitatis.* It begins in solemn and reverent tones; we are in the presence of the Lord. Yet the majestic chant of the archangels is cut off by the business-like, unfeeling intrusion of Mephisto's words. He speaks like the experienced manager of his own infernal enterprise whose success is measured by profit and loss. All else is illusion, including the circumstances of his own existence. In his conference with the Lord he says of Faust:

> Staub soll er fressen, und mit Lust,
> Wie meine Muhme, die berühmte Schlange.
> [334–35]

> Dust shall he eat, and that with pleasure,
> as did my relative, the celebrated snake.

"Berühmt?" Why famed, or why celebrated? God has no need to be informed of the serpent's illustrious place in theology. Nor need the spectator or reader be told that it is either famous or infamous. The name of the beast in a biblical context needs no further adjective. "Berühmt" is humorously redundant and creates another disillusioning wedge, for the idea of "fame" directs the mind both to deeds and their echoes through time and can be conceived only in a historical sense. But clearly, the conversation between the Lord and Mephisto is beyond time, as are also the hymns of the archangels and the wager between the Lord and Mephisto. They are eternal aspects of the theological cosmos, and as a result the word "berühmt" catapults the reader from his sojourn in the unchanging heavens into a crass social and historical reality. The gulf between the successive character of historical time and the eternal simultaneity in heaven is seemingly bridged by a linguistic sleight-of-hand.

Mephisto's last speech in the "Prologue" is more openly humorous, but it too contains a "double bottom" leading to unsuspected ironic depths:

> Von Zeit zu Zeit seh' ich den Alten gern,
> Und hüte mich, mit ihm zu brechen.
> Es ist gar hübsch von einem grossen Herrn,
> So menschlich mit dem Teufel selbst zu sprechen.
> [350–53]

> From time to time it's good to see the Old Man;
> I must be careful not to break with him.
> How decent of so great a personage
> to be so human with the devil.

Thomas Mann quoting these lines in his Princeton lecture "Goethe's Faust" (1938) comments: "Not for nothing have these two lines become so famous. Their humor is complex and subtle . . . a truly cosmic jest, a regular poet's joke, and very characteristic for this particular poet."[10] Mann left it at that, content to create an awareness of the complexity of this passage. The ambivalence of "menschlich" in reference to the Lord is obvious enough. It means "friendly, obliging," as well as "provided with human attributes." Obviously, both meanings in this case fail to satisfy; rather they contradict the requirements of the theological environment of the "Prologue." It is as if the public is being let in on a secret: "Let us drop all pretense in this talk about heaven. Let us speak man to man. I have set up a hypothetical situation for you, a category of the imagination, a playful parody of the Job story." The illusion of the stage is thus put into question even before Faust enters the scene, and the spectator is put on notice that he is about to witness a poetic experiment for which he himself must largely provide relevance and meaning.

Mephisto serves to break down fictions, including the fiction of the theater. The human need to reassemble the resulting scattered fragments into new meaningful relationships is a constant effective counterforce on which the poet may count so long as he is able to involve the spectator. Mephisto himself, "des Chaos wunderlicher Sohn," is a fragment of his former self; his realm of formlessness and death has been shattered by the event of God's creation:

Ich bin ein Teil des Teils, der anfangs alles war.
[1349]

I am a portion of the part which once was everything.

and his radical nihilism is evidence of his desire to reestablish the ancient, total supremacy of chaos. He is a single-minded figure who responds entirely to that aspect of nature which is susceptible to razor-sharp, rationalistic dissection, and who angrily or ironically dismisses irrational forces which are beyond his grasp. When in the end he is deprived of Faust's soul for whose possession he had labored so hard, he is full of righteous indignation: "Wer schafft mir mein erworbnes Recht?" ("Who will restore to me my well-earned right?") [l. 11833]. It cannot be denied that the devil has a strong case, for he had adhered fully to the terms of the contract, and Faust's questionable legal position has remained controversial to this day.[11] Mephisto's pathos in defeat is humorous, however, not only because he is a stock figure of church mystery plays and of the puppet theater, but also because the most ignominious defeat cannot diminish the power and meaning of his estate. He is, after all, not a flesh-and-blood character in the ordinary sense, and on several occasions he pointedly reminds the reader of this fact. For example, in his conversation with the young student who is eager to obtain authoritative advice concerning his future course of studies, he says: "Muss wieder recht den Teufel spielen" ("I must play the devil once again") (1. 2010), and when in the end his coveted prize, Faust's soul, is borne up by the angels whom he perversely finds sexually attractive, he refers to himself tautologically as "ein ausgepichter Teufel" ("a down-and-out devil")—making semantic fun of himself in a mock-serious vein. All this—with the lightest possible touch—confirms Mephisto as an eternal cosmic force without biography. His presence on the stage is concrete enough, but even as a poodle, a traveling scholar, or a Spanish nobleman, he represents the sovereign playfulness of a superior power to whom the world is a toy. With his brilliant invention of a crassly materialistic Mephisto, Goethe was able to bring each phase of Faust's development, and in fact the entire enterprise of dramatic representation, under the sharp light of criticism. The play thus contains a built-in dialectic between the opposites of poetry and non-poetry, meaning and non-meaning, life and death, God and devil.

Mephisto's illusion-destroying rationalism finds its embodiment in other contexts, though no other Goethean figure is gifted with Mephisto's cold perfection. It is easy to see why this should be so, for Mephisto is the manifestation of numerous powers endowed by theology with only a single essential function; hence, he is in-exorable and essentially uncomplicated. He is not a "character," but merely acts out a part assigned to him by tradition and a poet's imagination, as does the Lord. (See illustration, p. 72) When he does act like a human being—for example, when occasionally he makes a great show of being reluctant to serve Faust—this must be interpreted as an ironic adherence to his role on the popular stage. Goethe can therefore give his negative principle, concretely embodied though it may appear, the sharpness of an impersonal argument which nothing in the drama escapes; every affirmation is tested against its own denial.

Other characters in Goethe's works are materialistic and clever, but in a *human* way, i.e., their primary traits are crossed, softened, or obscured by the complexities of psychological motivations. In *Iphigenie*, the haunted and gloomy Orestes receives comfort from Pylades, a veritable paradigm of a steadfast friend and companion. Pylades is uncomplicated, rational, and cunning in ad-versity. His entire being is bent on rescuing his friends and himself from certain death at the hands of the barbaric king Thoas. He is able to cut through layers of distracting emotions and myths in order to grapple with the objective facts of the situation, and the lies and ruses which he proposes are necessary for the solution of difficult practical problems. Pylades is in the tradition of Greek colonizers, imbued with a conviction of Greek superiority. He stands in contrast to the complex and guilt-ridden Orestes and to his sister, Iphigenia, whose every action requires the sanction of an eighteenth-cen-tury moral code. By undercutting Pylades' strategy, she risks her life as well as that of her brother and companions, but the disarming strength of her honesty and of her "beautiful soul" soften the heart of the barbaric king. Thus the Greeks can depart as friends, and tragedy is averted through transcendence of factual reality. This conclusion resembles the end of the *Faust* drama, where the protagonist is saved through divine intervention, even though Mephisto could make a strong legal claim for Faust's soul. Pylades, in a sense, suffers a defeat somewhat analogous to Mephisto's, for the young Greek hero's keen awareness of factual reality proves inadequate when applied to characters whose humanity consists chiefly in never being quite predictable. Like Mephisto, Pylades occasionally undermines the poetic imagination to which he owes his existence, though unlike Mephisto he does it innocently. He is perfectly sincere when he expresses confidence in Apollo's oracle:

> Der Götter Worte sind nicht doppelsinnig
> Wie der Gedrückte sie im Unmut wähnt.
>
> [613–14]

> The words of Gods are not equivocal,
> As in despair the poor oppress'd one thinks.[12]

Only those who know the outcome of the drama can perceive the irony of his words, for much of the dramatic development hinges on misinterpretation of the oracle which Pylades had naively and piously regarded as unambiguous:

> "Bringst du die Schwester, die an Tauris' Ufer
> Im Heiligtume wider Willen bleibt,
> Nach Griechenland, so löset sich der Fluch."
>
> [2113–15]

> He answer'd "Back to Greece the sister bring,
> Who in the sanctuary on Tauris' shore
> Unwillingly abides; so ends the curse!"[13]

As we have seen earlier, Pylades' reminder to Orestes that one ought not to perform every deed with an eye to posthumous glory, is ironic and disillusioning in a sense similar to Mephisto's suggestion that Faust associate himself with a poet. What emerges is a play beyond a play, in which the stage becomes an avenue to a larger human drama whose theme is the struggle for an ever-heightening awareness of the relationship between subject and object. Much of the tragic aspect of the *Faust* drama—for Goethe consistently named it a tragedy—can be found in the titanic struggle and heroic failure to apprehend reality free from the ambiguities of analogies, symbols, and reflected images. Invariably the penetration of one illusion merely prepares for yet another one, even though this process is not always accompanied by irony. The majestic spectacle of the waterfall in whose surrounding mists the sun produces the colors of the rainbow serves to complete Faust's healing process at the beginning of *Faust II*. He is prepared to resume the quest implied by his wager with Mephistopheles. Thus in uttering the words "Am farbigen Abglanz haben wir das Leben" ("In mirrored hues we have our life and being") (1. 4727), he celebrates the glory and beauty of nature. It is also a moment of tragic resignation to his own insurmountable limits.

In this case, the abyss between the absolute and the circumscribed is stated in a tone of unironic nobility. The sun, the ultimate source of light, must blind the human eye, but its light, reflected on earth and refracted by vapors, produces the misty and many-colored domain of human nature. The rainbow arching over the waterfall is the symbol of reconciliation between gross, temporal matter and insubstantial eternity. The tragedy of Faust lies in his humanity; and the possibility of a transcendence by divine grace is within the compass of the poet's imagination.

NOTES

[1]*Gedenkausgabe* XVII, p. 707.

[2]*Dichtung und Wahrheit* II, p. 7.

[3]*Jubiläums.* III, p. 235.

[4]See also Ehrhard Bahr: "Aber das Unaussprechliche, Absolute, kann doch in Form der Ironie umschrieben und so erkennbar gemacht werden. In diesem Sinn ist Goethes Ironie als eine Ironie der Ehrfurcht zu verstehen." ". . . diese sehr ernsten Scherze . . .," *Jahrbuch der Goethe-Gesellschaft* XXXI [1969], p. 160)

[5]*Jubiläums.* VII, p. 215.

[6]*Jubiläums.* XIII, p. 205.

[7]Tr. Ben Kimpel and T. C. Duncan Eaves (Fayetteville, Ark., 1956), p. 23.

[8]Tr. Anna Swanwick (Philadelphia, n.d.), p. 37.

[9]Cf. *Odyssey* I, p. 303; III, p. 200; VIII, p. 580.

[10]*Essays of Three Decades*, tr. H. T. Lowe-Porter (New York, 1947), p. 28.

[11]See for example: Ada Klett, *Der Streit um Faust II seit 1900* (Jena, 1939); Harry Steinhauer, "Faust's Pact with the Devil," *PMLA* (March 1956), 180–200; Hermann Weigand, "Wetten und Pakt in Goethes Faust," *Monatshefte* (December, 1961), pp. 325–37.

[12]Tr. Anna Swanwick, op cit., p. 34.

[13]Ibid., p. 101.

3 • *Metamorphosis and Heightening*

As is the case of polarity, the images of metamorphosis are most explicitly present in the later additions to *Faust I* and in *Faust II.* Metamorphosis contains the notion of change as well as of sustained identity. It involves the unfolding of some of the myriad possibilities of an essence which is characterized and defined by a "concrete idea," a configuration which is knowable to a "delicate empiricism."[1] It is possible to devise a graphic representation showing the opposing lines of force which result in metamorphosis, though it must be understood that in contrast to polarity and intensification, metamorphosis is a *resultant* phenomenon. Polarity creates a precarious balance between plus and minus; intensification gives an upward direction to the series of transformations within that field of force. Transformations occur when a susceptible and creative human being runs the gamut of such archetypal forces.

A look at the diagram will show that at one extreme a character may move entirely along the negative route. Although he may undergo transformations, he will remain unaffected by opposing forces. The same is true of a character moving through events on the plus side of temporal events. The purely positive and purely negative

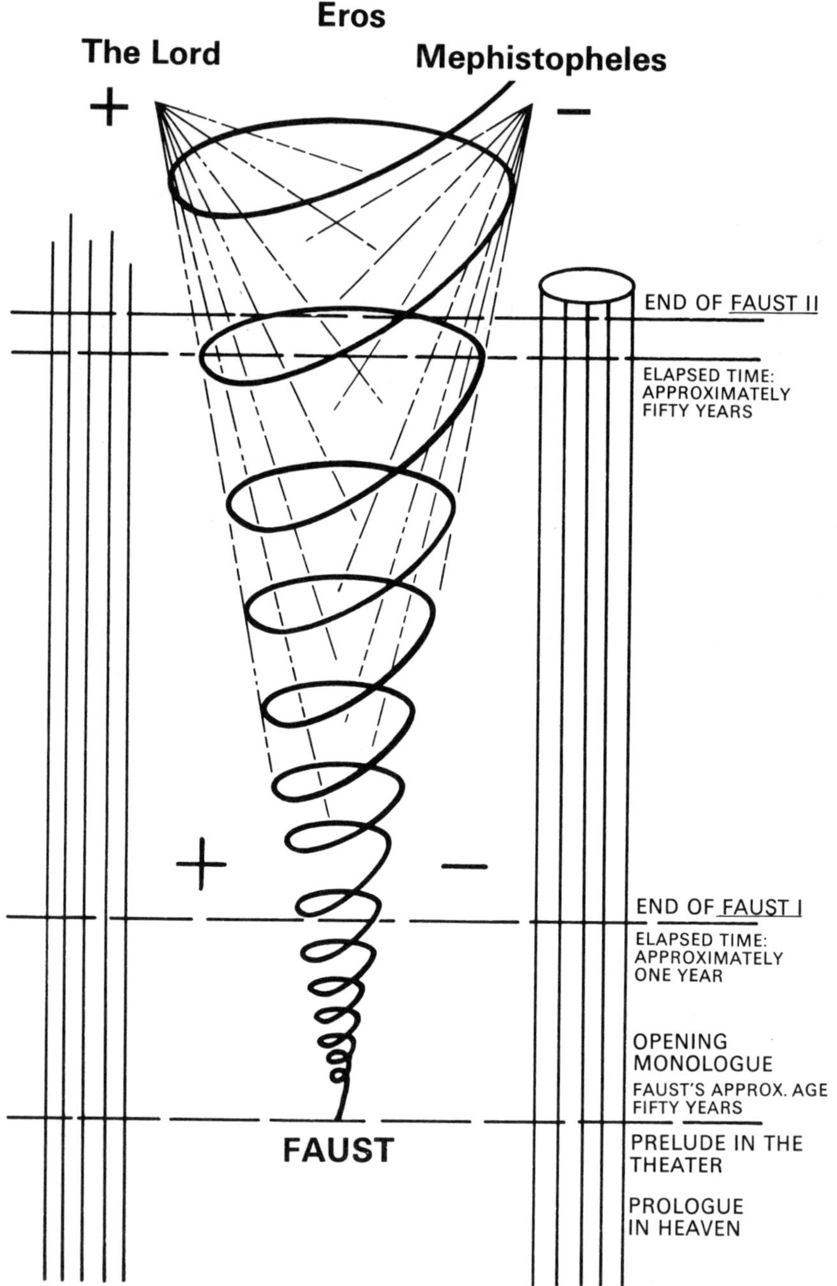

Faust's spiral course

routes are reserved for God and Satan, who remain unchanged by space or time. The biblical God suffers no embodiment and therefore no transformation; Mephisto's successive manifestations as Satan, poodle, club-footed devil, or classical Phorkias always add up to the same, eternal power that "wills evil and effects the good." Faust is in the middle of the cosmic scheme. Not Everyman, he yet embodies the utmost potential of man as a species, exposed to and in touch with numenous powers. His course winds between plus and minus, constantly circling the "right road" upward. It may be represented by a spiral along which are located the stations and transformations appropriate to his quest. Faust differs from the other characters in the drama: he is at all times developing and "heightening"—a process which, to be sure, includes pauses and even regressions—but the force and general direction of his striving are constant:

> Ein guter Mensch in seinem dunklen Drange
> Ist sich des rechten Weges wohl bewusst.
> [327–28]

> A good man in his dark and secret urgings
> is well aware which path to go.

The succeeding stages in Faust's development involve symbolic dying and symbolic rebirth, of which the near suicide and rejuvenation in Part I, the healing sleep and subsequent awakening in Part II, are important, though not the only examples. Each new stage in his life is a metamorphosis which contains within itself the meaning of past experience and the seeds of a higher stage of human definition. We noted earlier that the influences of archetypal forces upon the plant produced a "spiral tendency" (p. 27) which can now also be regarded as the most adequate metaphor for Faust's progress.

Certain figures in the drama, such as Mephisto and the sea-god Nereus, while they undergo transformations, do not exist in time. Appropriately, they are not heightened. Others are neither heightened nor transformed because they are insensitive and intractable to experience. They exist as personifications of their characters and know only to move through time in accordance with their designated roles. To this group belong Frau Marthe, Gretchen's hypocritical and mercenary neighbor, and Valentin, Gretchen's self-satisfied and narrow-minded soldier-brother.

At least one character is heightened without moving through a spiral course and without metamorphosis, but through the straight and direct route, which man cannot long endure. This route to super-human transcendence leads inexorably to disaster: the child Euphorion, inheriting overpowering endowments from Faust and Helena, wishes to be an Icarus, and is smashed at the foot of the cliff from which he leaps.

It would be no easy task to fit all characters into our scheme. I am thinking primarily of the difficulty of seeing Gretchen in this way, for she does not really undergo transformations until after her death. She is self-contained, intellectually unassuming, and content within her limits. Seen from a higher level, however, she is a manifestation of the "eternal feminine" whose ultimate "flowering" occurs in the Catholic heaven at the end of *Faust II.* Looking at Gretchen in this manner, however, does not mean failing to do full justice to her as a character; rather; it makes it possible to see her as a structural element in the total configuration of the drama.

As with polarity, however, metamorphosis and heightening are also structural elements of the drama itself, identifiable by the steadily increasing scope of the subject matter which typically progresses by mirror reflections; by the traversing of ever larger segments of time; by the orbits of meaning which expand until in the end they break out of earthly contexts to dwell on the symbolic representation of heaven. Indeed, it seems impossible to provide a complete list of structural equivalents to metamorphosis and heightening because literally every poetic line can be seen as part of such a list. Each can be considered an organic aspect of an overall pattern. If one begins with language and poetic manner, one could point to the ironic style and see in the progression from satire to irony an analogous heightening of poetry until in the final scene in heaven there is not a mere heightening, but a transcendence of irony into cosmic worship, and of metaphorical indirection into direct statement, of language into choral music:

> CHORUS MYSTICUS:
> Alles Vergängliche
> Ist nur ein Gleichnis;
> Das Unzulängliche,
> Hier wird's Ereignis;
> Das Unbeschreibliche,
> Hier ist's getan;
> Das Ewig-Weibliche
> Zieht uns hinan.

> CHORUS MYSTICUS:
> All things corruptible
> Are but a parable;
> Earth's insufficiency
> Here finds fulfillment;

> Here the ineffable
> Wins life through love;
> Eternal Womanhood
> Leads us above.

The matter of the progressive stages of Faust's dramatic life can be assigned to form or content; they are at home in either: as an integral part of the drama's structural development or as an entity—an "entelechy" in Leibnitzean terms—or ever-heightening human scope and cosmic relevance. Within the compass of the two major stages of Faust's development there are relatively minor transformations which are in all cases both *results* of surrounding forces, and themselves the forces behind future developments. The Faust in Part II is not the same as the earlier protagonist. Intellectual brashness, absolutistic demands, and Don Juanism have given way to imaginative circumspection; the breath-taking activity of the Earth Spirit's conjurer, seducer of Gretchen and ever-frustrated besieger of the heavens, is put to rest on the soft grass of an alpine meadow. What had been pathetic, tragic, human and inhuman has now been demoted from the surface to lower regions of consciousness. In other words, *Faust I* has become poetic material for *Faust II*. It is absorbed, commented, and acted upon. The new poetry is poetry poeticized. The very first scene shows a regenerated Faust, resigned to the limitations of a human predicament which had been synonymous with imprisonment. But the new Faust is not humbled into a life which is second best. He has, on the contrary, emerged with new faculties for growth.[2] These faculties are no longer used to break down barriers by frontal assault, but instead to bring him to a condition of poetic integrity and activity which in the end is worthy of divine grace.

Faust's state at the beginning of the drama is so crude that he lacks understanding even of his human limits. He is able to conjure the Earth Spirit, but fails to stand up to its overpowering presence. Propelled by the "cruder juices" of his spirit, his growth and progress occur by successive stages. He is not sufficiently refined to experience the "flowering" of simultaneity. As the Spirit describes its function and proceeds to define itself, Faust becomes aware of his inferiority to even this lower member of the world of spirits. He moves from ecstatic joy to deep despondency during the confrontation. Just when Faust joyfully proclaims his own kinship with the Spirit, he is devastated by the words:

> Du gleichst dem Geist, den du begreifst.
> Nicht mir!
>
> [512–13]

> You're like the spirit that you grasp.
> You're not like me!

This pronouncement, not usually commented upon in editions of *Faust*, shows the hero at the lowest level of his existence. The hitherto somewhat grandiose magician is crushed by the obvious truth of the Spirit's words and exclaims in despair:

> Ich Ebenbild der Gottheit!
> Und nicht einmal Dir!

> I, the image of the godhead!
> And not your equal?

Faust's thoughts soon turn to suicide as an escape from

life's futility. The Spirit's words remarkably reflect an often stated principle in Goethe's natural philosophy, most notably in the Introduction to his *Theory of Color:* "In this connection we are reminded of the old Ionian School which stated many times and with great emphasis that equality can be recognized only by what is equal. . . ."[3] This is followed by four lines which poetically render the comments of "mystical" Plotinus on the resemblance between the sun and the human eye (p. 135).

Equipped with this information, we can read the Earth Spirit's lines somewhat as follows: "You, Faust, have not yet developed a sense capable of reaching me. You are still far away from the level of 'higher contemplation' at which I can be grasped. You must develop and acquire this sense through progressive transformations before you can hope to countenance me: 'You're like the spirit that you grasp,/You're not like me.'"

NOTES

[1]See p. 14.

[2]See also pp. 114–115.

[3]"Hierbei erinnern wir uns der alten ionischen Schule, welche mit so grosser Bedeutsamkeit immer wiederholte, nur von Gleichem werde gleiches erkannt, . . ." *(Hamb. Ausg.* XIII, p. 324).

4 • *Eros and Knowledge*

The inquiry into the principles of polarity, metamorphosis, and heightening and their functions in the *Faust*
poem has shown that "heightening" tends to be qualitatively somewhat different from the others because of its
association with movement and direction. The German
word *Steigerung* used by Goethe, as well as our translation of it as "heightening," indicate that the movement
is upward in the archetypal sense that all development
and perfection is "up," and that crude and unformed matter is "down." Purgatory is a terraced mountain, and
the flight to the Empyrean is up. Goethe saw fit to
symbolize Faust's upward path most emphatically in the
last scene of the drama. In medieval church-play fashion, the angels snatch Faust's soul from under Mephisto's
nose and carry it into the heavens, where souls move
about at their assigned altitudes. Before this scene,
Faust's earthly "upward" development is implicit in the
image evoked by growth, perennially engraved in our
minds as upward-directed. Yet, on the other hand, Faust's
explicit movements are by no means always upward:
the students in Auerbach's cellar to whom he and Mephisto pay a memorable visit entertain themselves on as low
a plane as is rather obviously implied by their location

just below street level. Faust also descends to the Witch's Kitchen, and he probes deeply into the roots of Being during his mystic quest for the Mothers.

Nor do Faust's sojourns at physical heights always bring him into contact with correspondingly higher or recondite psychic states. The ascent to the Brocken allows him to view the spectacle of the Witch's Sabbath and brings him to the most desperate and hopeless moment of his quest.

To attach the attributes "high" or "low" to all of Faust's experience leads to oversimplification and even falsification. Each experience is digested and transformed by Faust's complex and churning psyche which cannot help but expand and grow. This is the pressure from within. There is, however, from the "Prologue in Heaven" to the final ascent to Heaven, a corresponding force from without, an archetypal power drawing all things to itself, which one is tempted to call God, or His emanations, or His Host. One is forced to make a distinction between the impetuous upward push of a Faust who is dreaming of flight, or Euphorions's Icarus-misadventure, and on the other hand, a more gentle drawing upward as part of an organic development. In Faust's world, physical flight is connected with black magic and dream-like visions, or with a breaking of human bonds, and typically leads to catastrophe. Growth, by contrast, is the natural, most essential gift of man. Faust's striving is ennobled and sanctified by nature. There is an encounter between a longing from within and a loving response from without, a motif which is present in several of Goethe's poems. Its prototype is "Ganymed," composed as early as 1774, which contains the seeds of much that is to come:

Wie im Morgenrot   1
Du rings mich anglühst,
Frühling, Geliebter!
Mit tausendfacher Liebeswonne
Sich an mein Herz drängt   5
Deiner ewigen Wärme
Heilig Gefühl,
Unendliche Schöne!

Dass ich dich fassen möcht'
An diesen Arm!   10

Ach, an deinem Busen
Lieg' ich, schmachte,
Und deine Blumen, dein Gras
Drängen sich an mein Herz.
Du kühlst den brennenden   15
Durst meines Busens,
Lieblicher Morgenwind,
Ruft drein die Nachtigall
Liebend nach mir aus dem Nebeltal.

Ich komme! Ich komme!   20
Wohin? Ach, wohin?

Hinauf, hinauf strebst's,
Es schweben die Wolken
Abwärts, die Wolken
Neigen sich der sehnenden Liebe,   25
Mir, Mir!

In Euerm Schosse
Aufwärts!
Umfangend umfangen!
Aufwärts   30
An deinem Busen,
Alliebender Vater!

How sunrise-red   1
You glow at me,
O Spring, my beloved!
With thousandfold ecstasy
The holy thrall   5
Of your infinite warmth
Inundates my heart,
Eternal Beauty!

That I could grasp you
In this very arm!   10
Ah, at your breast
I lie, languish,
And your flowers, your grasses
Invade my heart.
You soothe the burning   15
Thirst within me,
Caressing morning breeze;
A nightingale makes loving intrusion,
From the misty dale below.

I'm coming! I'm coming!   20
Where? Ah, where?

Upward, upward rising;
And downward gliding,
Downward the clouds,
Drawn to love and yearning,   25
To me, to me!

By you enfolded
Upward
Embraced and embracing!
Upward   30
At your side,
All-loving Father!

The ecstatic bliss evoked in these famous stanzas of free

Storm and Stress verse is not crossed by any hint of resignation or possible shipwreck. Ganymede is after all a mythological figure and *not* a Werther or Faust enmeshed in his society and his human self.

In 1819, the motif appears once more in "Selige Sehnsucht," this time enfolded in a series of related images:

Sagt es niemand, nur den Weisen,   1
Weil die Menge gleich verhöhnet,
Das Lebend'ge will ich preisen,
Das nach Flammentod sich sehnet.

In der Liebesnächte Kühlung,   5
Die dich zeugte, wo du zeugtest,
Überfällt dich fremde Fühlung,
Wenn die still Kerze leuchtet.

Nicht mehr bleibest du umfangen
In der Finsternis Beschattung,   10
Und dich reisset neu Verlangen
Auf zu höherer Begattung.

Keine Ferne macht dich schwierig,
Kommst geflogen und gebannt,
Und zuletzt, des Lichts begierig,   15
Bist du, Schmetterling, verbrannt.

Und so lang du das nicht hast,
Dieses: Stirb und werde!
Bist du nur ein trüber Gast
Auf der dunklen Erde.   20

Tell it no one, for the crowd   1
Is given to quick mockery.

Only to the wise I'll praise the life
That yearns for death in fire.

In the coolness of the lovers' night   5
That once begat you where you now beget;
You're overwhelmed by otherness,
While the quiet candle shines.

No longer do you rest
In the gentle shades of night.   10
A new precipitous desire
Spurs you on to higher consummation.

And no distance is a hindrance,
You fly and are transfixed,
And in the end, in craving light,   15
O moth, you are consumed by it.

So long as you have not acquired
This: Die and then be born again!
You are but a murky tenant
Upon a gloomy earth.   20

These poems show how the upward movement is accompanied and furthered by love. All traditional fortunes
and misfortunes associated with eros radiate their meaning on the progression leading toward the "higher consummation" (1. 12) of a transcendent embrace. In
"Ganymed" the "I" is swept up and carried to its blissful
destination which is reached with the line "Umfangend
umfangen" (1. 29); and here at the poem's culmination
the direct coupling of a present and past participle evokes
a startling moment of verbal alchemy. Where before there
had been both upward and downward motion—the clouds
reaching down to meet the upward-yearning youth—now
there is only one upward thrust of two perfectly fused
energies.

The "You" in the more contemplative "Selige Sehnsucht," which Goethe wrote when he was almost seventy, also moves upward, but by no means in a straight line. It must die and be reborn and transformed along the way. Death and rebirth, "Stirb and werde" (1. 18), have become the imperative adjuncts of a circuitous upward development. The symbolic range of the sexual embrace is expanded to include pain and death and even didactic aloofness in the last stanza.

Similarly each regression along Faust's journey of experience is a "sterben," a kind of death and precursor of a higher subsequent metamorphosis. Thus Faust's emergence at the beginning of Part II from the spiritual death of his guilt toward Gretchen and his expanded vision in a larger world, calls to mind the "werden" of "Selige Sehnsucht." The moods of "Ganymed" and "Selige Sehnsucht" alternate throughout the drama, with the coolness and wisdom of the latter gradually gaining the upper hand.

How many and precisely what kind of transformations Faust undergoes is subject to varying interpretations and controversy because it is difficult to draw lines of demarcation. As a working hypothesis, the five stages proposed by Ernst Jockers and H. Rickert[1] appear acceptable, so long as their provisional nature is understood: the "mystic-pantheistic" phase up to Faust's drinking of the witch's brew; the "sensualist-erotic" phase of the Gretchen episode; the "aesthetic" phase culminating in the Helena act (act III) of Part II; the "socio-ethical" phase delimited by acts IV and V, up to Faust's burial; and the "religious and erotic" phase at the end of act V. True enough, the singling out of such successively dominant stages in Faust's dramatic existence tends to draw the attention

away from the ambivalence and ephemeral quality of each
of these phases. Yet as signposts to underlying complexities they reliably indicate the path to be followed.[2]

Keeping in mind Faust's predicament in the opening
monologue we may ask ourselves the legitimate question "What is *Faust* about?" and then bravely answer
"*Faust* is about knowledge." This is a one-sided reply,
but at least it has the virtue of not being false. Moreover,
the notion of the quest for knowledge gives us the corre-
lation for Faust's upward movement we have been seek-
ing. In the two poems just cited, upward movement is
associated with eros, and I think it can be shown that
Faust's quest for knowledge is inseparable from eros in
all its forms. It is characteristic of Goethe to show the
relevance of age-old myths in the context of his own poetry and of his own heightened sensibility—and therefore
not surprising that knowledge in the biblical sense is
closely associated in *Faust* with sexuality. In fact, Goethe
places the central image of the Tree of Knowledge in a
somewhat peripheral scene during Walpurgis Night.
The presence of screeching hags presided over by Satan
himself, and Faust's own oppressive vision of Gretchen
with a cord around her neck "no broader than a razor's
edge," provide the setting of guilt, more precisely, sexual
guilt. The lines referred to are sung alternately by Faust
and the beautiful young witch Lilith, the succuba of ancient rabbinic tradition:

FAUST:
    Einst hatt' ich einen schönen Traum:
    Da sah ich einen Apfelbaum,
    Zwei schöne Äpfel sah ich dran,
    Sie reizten mich, ich stieg hinan.

                       [4128–31]

> Once I fell to pleasant dreaming:
> I saw a sturdy apple tree,
> With two apples on it gleaming—
> I climbed it for they tempted me.

In the following stanza, Faust's "lovely dream" is interpreted by his brazen and lustful partner in the same ominously playful meter and rhyme:

DIE SCHÖNE
> Der Äpfelchen begehrt ihr sehr,
> Und schon vom Paradiese her.
> Von Freuden fühl' ich mich bewegt,
> Dass auch mein Garten solche trägt.

[4132–35]

> You want apples of a pleasing size;
> You've looked for them since paradise.
> I am thrilled with joy and pleasure,
> for my garden holds such treasure.

In a prose paraphrase this could be rendered somewhat as follows: "The apples which you seek are my breasts; they are the forbidden fruit from the Tree of Knowledge which you, the paradigm of man, have never ceased wanting to enjoy. Adam and Eve's loss of sexual innocence is the eternal concomitant of such knowledge." Unequivocally, Goethe in this suggestive ditty relates the desire for "forbidden" knowledge with sexuality and a sense of guilt.

It seems almost as though Goethe poetically anticipated what in our age has become a tenet of existential psychology. In *L'Etre et le néant* (1943) we read the description of what Jean-Paul Sartre has chosen to call the Actaeon complex:

Every investigation implies the idea of nudity which one brings out into the open by clearing away the obstacles which cover it, just as Actaeon clears away the branches so that he can have a better view of Diana at her bath. More than this, knowledge is a hunt. Bacon called it the hunt of Pan. The scientist is the hunter who surprises a white nudity and who violates it by looking at it.

. . . In addition, the idea of discovery, of revelation, includes an idea of appropriative enjoyment. What is seen is possessed; to see is to deflower.[3]

Faust's tragic union with Gretchen is a way station along his quest for absolute knowledge, as is also his phantasmagoric encounter with Helena. In *Faust* sexual embrace is an analogy as well as the supreme instance of this knowledge, a merger between subject and object, as well as a synthesis between two poles. Knowledge is thus the "highest activity." To embrace nature in its temporal and spatial aspects in a single supreme moment, to penetrate its "open mysteries," is the function of eros.

Basing himself on imagery so old and universally, if unconsciously, accepted that it has entered the language of everyday discourse, Goethe employs the attributes of dryness, dustiness, and brittleness to connote futility and frustration. Thus the paraphernalia of learning with which Faust is surrounded in his Gothic cell, are parched and dead. The more he becomes aware of the dryness and dust about him, the greater becomes his longing for moisture and the flow of life. While enthralled by the Sign of the Macrocism, he exclaims:

> Ha! Welche Wonne f l i e s s t in diesem Blick
> Auf einmal mir durch alle meine Sinnen!
>
> [430–41]

    Ha! A rush of bliss
    flows suddenly through all my senses!

and

    Auf, b a d e , Schüler, unverdrossen
    Dir ird'sche Brust im Morgenrot!*

[445–46]

    Pupil, stand up and unafraid
    bathe your earthly breast in morning light!

In the first part of the drama, Faust consistently expresses his yearning by invoking images of succulence and flowing saps:

    Man sehnt sich nach des Lebens Bächen,
    Ach! nach des Lebens Quelle hin!

[1200–01]

    We crave to hold within our grasp
    the streams of life and, ah, its sources!

At the beginning of the Walpurgis Night, when he wanders with Mephisto through the Harz mountains, the images of liquidity he uses and those of dry iciness of his companion contrast strikingly:

FAUST

    Was hilft's, dass man den Weg verkürzt!—
    Im Labyrinth der Täler hinzuschleichen,
    Dann diesen Felsen zu ersteigen,
    Von dem der Quell sich ewig sprudelnd stürzt,
    Das ist die Lust, die solche Pfäde würzt !

*Letter spacing for emphasis in this and the previous quotation is mine.

MEPHISTO

> Fürwahr, ich spüre nichts davon!
> Mir ist es winterlich im Leibe,
> Ich wünschte Schnee und Frost auf meiner Bahn.
> Wie traurig steigt die unvollkommne Scheibe
> Des roten Monds mit später Glut heran,[4]
>
> · · · · · · · · · · · · · · ·　　　　[3840–52]

FAUST

> Why should I want to shorten the excursion?
> To creep along the labyrinthine valleys,
> then to scale this sudden towering cliff,
> eternal source of spurting, plunging waters—
> those are the tingling pleasures of such trails!

MEPHISTO

> Myself I notice no such thing.
> I feel winter in my bone and marrow
> and look for snow and frost to line my path.
> How sadly the unfinished, lunar disc
> emerges with belated, ruddy glow,
>
> · · · · · · · · · · · · ·

Nor is it difficult to find similar juxtapositions in Part II. The first scene shows Faust asleep and dreaming; friendly spirits conspire to heal his wounds of guilt and frustration by providing forgetfulness and by directing his glance toward the future. They chant of spring, and looking upon their sleeping charge, command their subordinate spirits:

> Erst senkt sein Haupt auf kühle Polster nieder.
> Dann badet ihn im Tau aus Lethe's Flut;
>
> 　　　　　　　　　　　　　　[4628–29]

> Pillow his head upon the sweet, cool lawn,
> Then bathe his limbs with dew from Lethe's lea;

In the "Classical Walpurgis Night," Homunculus, the glass-enclosed creature made in the crucibles of Wagner's laboratory, is shown longing for biological life. The philosopher Thales in a magnificent operatic scene exclaims:

> Alles ist aus dem Wasser entsprungen!!
> Alles wird durch das Wasser erhalten!
> Ozean, gönn uns dein ewiges Walten.
>
> [8435–37]

> From the wave was all created.
> Water will all life sustain:
> Ocean, grant your endless reign!

And Homunculus, "seduced" by Proteus, is drawn to Galatea, the most glorious of the Nereids riding in triumph on a sea shell, until he breaks his glass container, pours out its substance and unites with the goddess. Homunculus, by "its" destruction, is paradoxically thrust into the realm of true being. This scene contains the most explicit association of water with sexuality, where the words reflect the essence of the sexual embrace:

THALES
> Homunculus ist es, von Proteus verführt—
> Es sind die Symptome des herrischen Sehnens,
> Mir ahnet das Ächzen beängsteten Dröhnens;
> Er wird sich zerschellen am glänzenden Thron;
> Jetzt flammt es, nun blitzt es, ergiesset sich schon.

SIRENEN
> Welch feuriges Wunder verklärt uns die Wellen,
> Die gegeneinander sich funkelnd zerschellen?
>
> . . . .
>
> So herrsche denn Eros, der alles begonnen!
>
> [8469–79]

THALES
> Homunculus this, whom old Proteus misleads—

And the signs show the longing and will of their master,
Boding the pangs and the moans of disaster;
His glass will be shivered against the bright throne;
Comes a flame and a flash, on the floods he is strown.
SIRENS
The waves are transfigured with fire-laden wonder,
They glitter in impact, in flame-leap asunder.

. . . .

Let Eros who wrought it be honoured and crowned!

In the last act, there is another return to water. The accumulating sediments from the oceanic surf are ultimately turned into new and fertile coastal lands by means of human ingenuity and the directed labor of masses of people.

The figures of dryness recede somewhat in *Faust II*. The hero has come a long way since he left his parchments and dusty instruments, but the familiar images of dryness return whenever the distant past is invoked. For example, Faust's former study, the "high-vaulted Gothic chamber," to which he temporarily returns at the beginning of the second act, reintroduces the old imagery. When Mephisto draws the bellstrap, a new famulus appears who fearfully notes the ominous vibrations and tremblings caused by his unaccustomed presence:

> Springt das Estrich, und von oben
> Rieselt Kalk und Schutt verschoben.
>
> [6624–25]
>
> Floor is warped with wrack and trouble,
> Pouring down comes lime and rubble.

and then goes on to describe his red-eyed and scorched master, Wagner, who has meanwhile become an important alchemist in his own right:

Er sieht aus wie ein Kohlenbrenner,
Geschwärzt vom Ohre bis zur Nasen,
Die Augen rot vom Feuerblasen,
So lechzt er jeden Augenblick;

[6677–80]

You'd think he lived by charcoal-burning.
Nose and ears all sooty-smeared,
Eyes from the bellows red and bleared,
He toils through hours with choking lungs;

But on the whole, "moisture" is more abundant in *Faust II*, both in figures of speech and in explicit statements. The argument between Thales and Anaxagoras, i.e., between "Neptunism" and "Vulcanism," is won by Thales, who propounds that water is the basic forming element, and lost by Anaxagoras, who is here presented as believing that the fiery and eruptive forces of nature are responsible for the shape and character of the world.

We may say that Faust's frustration and despondency in the opening monologue stems from the dryness and sterility of his life. Correspondingly, Faust's longing for "wetness" is associated with life, creative activity, and outright sexuality:

Wo fass' ich dich, unendliche Natur?
Euch Brüste, wo? Ihr Quellen alles Lebens,
An denen Himmel und Erde hängt,
Dahin die welke Brust sich drängt—
Ihr quellt, ihr tränkt, und schmacht' ich so vergebens?

[455–59]

Where shall I clasp you, infinity of Nature?
You breasts, where? You wellsprings of all life?
Heaven and earth depend on you—
Toward you my parched soul is straining.
You flow, you nourish, yet I crave in vain.

These lines are of special interest because the image of breasts and embrace has its close analogy in the seduction scene between Faust and Gretchen:

> Ach, kann ich nie
> Ein Stündchen ruhig dir am Busen hängen,
> Und Brust an Brust und Seel' in Seele drängen?
> [3502–04]

> Oh, shall I never
> hang upon your bosom one short hour,
> pressing breast on breast, my soul into your soul?

Moisture and sexuality occur also in the form of a cruel parody in Auerbach's Cellar. The reveling and raucous students find a momentary shallow bliss in the illusion of flowing, precious wines and green foliage conjured up before them by Mephisto's tricks, a vision which dissolves into a leaping flame of hellfire as the devil shows his true identity. The image of liquidity and succulent grapes is nevertheless effective, though it is a parody that shows up the crudeness of the low life to which Faust has been exposed. Each of the three stanzas of the "Song of the Rat," moreover, rendered boisterously by one of the revelers, ends with the refrain in which the entire group joins "als hätt' sie Lieb im Leibe" ("As if she had love in her belly") (1. 2132, 2140, 2148). The rat is in agony from the poison it has swallowed and frantically looks for puddles of water, but to no avail. Her condition is described by the venomous colloquialism "sie pfeift auf dem letzten Loch" ("This is her final toot") (1. 2147). Suddenly and unexpectedly the refrain connects the cruelty of the song with the lethal capacities of sex, and only in retrospect does one realize that the filthy water by which the rat seeks salvation is a grotesque inversion of the restorative qualities which had hitherto been associated with wetness. Thus the song foreshadows Gretchen's disaster brought on by Faust and engineered by Mephistopheles.[5]

However, it is not only images of liquidity that invariably conjure up natural growth and sexuality. Other symbolic devices in *Faust* lend further subliminal strength to sexuality, such as one of the most important myths Goethe ever created, contained in the final scenes of the first act of *Faust II*. Here Faust is magically conveyed beyond time and space to the realm of the Mothers from which he will draw Helen of Troy and Paris into the concreteness of the present. It is a sleight of hand and, as the poet frequently reminds us, a common stage trick. Faust, upon hearing the word "Mother," experiences the awe and creative tremor which in other contexts Goethe reserved for the encounter with the "open mystery" of the *Urphäno-men* ["Das Schaudern ist der Menschheit bestes Teil" ("A shuddering awe shows what is best in man") (1. 6272).]*

The casual observation that the key in Faust's hand is a phallic symbol—rather obvious in our Freudian age—seems too facile and untrustworthy. Yet, sufficient evidence is available which strongly suggests that the Freudian interpretation is indeed correct and that it adds another significant dimension to the scene.

Faust is forced into a quest for Helena not only because the emperor wishes to be entertained, but because a desire for her had become part of his being when he saw an image of feminine perfection in the Witch's Kitchen. At that time Mephisto's comment was:

---

*Translation is mine.

Du siehst, mit diesem Trank im Leibe,
Bald Helenen in jedem Weibe.

[2603–04]

With that potion in your belly
You'll soon see Helena in every wench.

Indeed, Faust remembers at what point in his own distant past such an imperious force was released, for he says to Mephisto:

Die Wohlgestalt, die mich voreinst entzückte,
In Zauberspiegelung beglückte,
War nur ein Schaumbild solcher Schöne!

[6495–97]

That comely form enchanting once my mind,
That mirrored magic joy of womankind,
Was but a pale foam-phantom of such beauty.

The key in Faust's hand is to help him seek out and gain access to the realm of the Mothers and to draw Helena away from the prison of her past. Somewhat surprisingly, the key is small, causing Faust to exclaim: "Das kleine Ding!" ("That petty thing") (1. 6259), but it grows immediately in his hand and becomes strangely luminous. Faust then wields it with great authority as he approaches the Mothers. His disappearance causes concern even to Mephisto, who feels impelled in this exceptional moment to speak the truth as a last resort. A little more than one hundred lines later, Faust has returned, and as he touches a luminous basin with the key, Paris and Helena enter the stage, acting out their play for the entertainment of the king and his court. In an instant of dramatic irony, Mephisto (from the prompter's box) admonishes the ecstatic Faust, now dressed in priestly robes: "So fasst euch doch und fallt nicht aus der Rolle!" ("Be careful or you'll overstep your part!") (l. 6501). Helena and Paris re-enact their mythological past, while the stage audience comments on the action. Helena approaches the sleeping youth, bends over and kisses him. Paris awakens to his stature as a Greek hero, boldly embraces Helena and proceeds to carry her off. Faust, beside himself with jealousy, turns the key toward Paris—whereupon the entire stage illusion collapses in the puff of a magical explosion. The mythical figures have vanished and Faust lies unconscious on the stage.

In the most important prose work of Goethe's old age, *Wilhelm Meisters Wanderjahre*, which like the "Mothers" scene in *Faust* was written during the last decade of his life, a key again plays an important role. The scene occurs during an episode in the second chapter of the third book as an integral part of the love story between Hersilie and Felix. In a letter to Wilhelm Meister, Hersilie tells how "a good or evil spirit" drove her to find a key:

> Ein winzig kleines, stachlichtes Etwas kommt mir in die Hand; ich, die ich sonst so apprehensiv, kitzlich und schreckhaft bin, schliesse die Hand, schliesse sie, schweige, . . . Sogleich ergriff mich von allen Empfindungen die wunderlichste. Beim ersten verstohlenen Blick seh ich, errat' ich, zu Ihrem Kästchen sei es der Schlüssel.[6]

> A tiny prickly something comes into my hand; I who am usually so apprehensive, ticklish, and nervous, close my hand around it, close it and remain silent, . . . I was immediately seized by the strangest possible sensation. At the first furtive glimpse, I saw, I knew that it was the key to your jewel box.

Hersilie includes a drawing of the key in her letter:

and beneath it, she adds:

> Hier aber, mein Freund, nun schliesslich zu dieser Ab-
> bildung des Rätsels was sagen Sie, erinnert es nicht an
> Pfeile mit Widerhaken? Gott sei uns gnädig[7]

> But here, my friend, what do you say to the puzzle pic-
> tured here—does it not conjure up arrows with barbed
> hooks? May God help us!

Much later in the book, Hersilie writes another letter
to Wilhelm, this time giving an account of a visit by
Felix. She describes how "like a young god" he had appeared and how she had teasingly shown him the key to
a mysterious jewel casket. Felix had implored her to give
him the key, had fallen on his knees before her and de-
clared his love. In a moment of weakness, Hersilie let
him seize the key from her hand, whereupon Felix ex-
claimed triumphantly:

> Ich habe nichts vom Kästchen noch vom Schlüssel!
> . . . Dein Herz wünscht' ich zu öffnen, dass es sich mir
> auftäte, mir entgegenkäme, mich an sich drückte, mir
> vergönnte, es an meine Brust zu drücken.
>
> [III, 17][8]

> The jewel box and key can do nothing for me! . . .
> It's your heart I wish to unlock, so it would open to me,
> meet me, press me to it and allow me to press it against
> my breast.

Carried along by his passion, Hersilie allowed him to
embrace her, only to reget it the next instant. She angrily
wheeled upon him, commanding him never to come before her eyes again. Felix turned abruptly, uttering in
bitter despair: "Gut, so reit' ich in die Welt bis ich
umkomme" ("Good, then I'll ride into the world until I
perish").

Although the scenes of Faust's confrontation with the
Mothers and Hersilie's encounter with Felix are vastly
different in scope and character, there are enough specific similarities to justify a comparison. In both cases,
a point is made of the smallness of the key. The prose
and greater realism of the *Wanderjahre* preclude the
phantasmagoric flights which we accept quite readily in
the mystical and twice-removed atmosphere of the Faustian play within a play. Yet there is a hint of magic and
mystery in the prose episode as well, which comes to
the reader indirectly through physical and psychological
reactions. Hersilie's letter is, on the whole, written in the
balanced, leisurely style of a report, but the account of
the key is fraught with excitement, conveyed by short,
breathless sentences and many points of exclamation and
interrogation:

> Gott sei uns gnädig! . . . Und nun mädchenhaft genug
> noch eine Nachschrift! Was geht aber mich und Sie
> eigentlich das Kästchen an?   [III, 2][9]

God help us! . . . And now for a girlish enough postscript: What actually does the jewel box have to do with you and me?

While she does not know what secret the key is meant to unlock, Hersilie feels intuitively and under the guidance of a "good or evil spirit" that it will fit the mysterious casket. In keeping with her lighthearted nature, she is driven by curiosity *(Neugier)*. Could one not assume that such curiosity is to Hersilie what the titanic search for knowledge and experience is to Faust? In both instances, the secret to which the key is intended to give access is equal to, or symbolically associated with, the feminine principle. As we have seen, Felix is not interested in either the key or the jewel box, but only in their symbolically erotic values, and Faust's key not only guides its owner to nature's matrix but, in addition, has the power to draw the paradigm of all femininity, Helena, to the here and now of poetic reality. And finally, in both scenes, misjudgment and a failure of restraint bring on catastrophe.

The allegorical use of the key as an instrument capable of unlocking tender secrets is probably nearly as old as the invention of its purely mechanical model. Goethe uses its conventional associations, expands and enriches them, and as a result the key glows in the light of symbolized Eros and mythology, or Eros and psychology. Hersilie notes that the tiny, bristly something resembles a barbed arrow, and although the arrow belongs to the rococo arsenal of amorous weapons, in this passage it lacks the playfully allegorical air so typical of that period. The clusters of meaning surrounding the key and the arrow are merged into one of unusual density and scope. In a lyrical stanza composed by the aged Goethe between

1819 and 1823 under the impact of his encounter with young Ulrike von Levetzow, the arrow functions as a symbol of hurtful passion, used with the originality of an immediate experience.

Denn freilich sind's dergleichen Kiel' und Pfeile,
Die, hin und wieder fliegend, würkend zischen,
Gehetzt in Eile, bogenhaft in Weile
In tausendfält'gem Wollen sich vermischen.
Man weiss nicht, soll man? Oder soll's verschieben?—
Nur wer sich kennt, der hat das Recht zu lieben.[10]

There are indeed such quills and arrows
which sailing and hissing do their work,
racing to their goal or arching leisurely,
tangled in thousandfold desire.
You hesitate. Should you, now? Or should you yet postpone?
You must know yourself to have the right to love.

The close functional association, almost identity, of the key and the arrow, leads to the conclusion that the key in Faust's hand as he is about to embark on his journey to the Mothers, is more than a "substitute for a magician's wand."[11] It is an erotic symbol and, as such, part of the central force of the drama.[12]

We must be careful not to assimilate the analogy between eros and knowledge into a positivistic or rigidly causative system, but rather to view it as a datum for a "delicate empiricism." For surely to relate all aspects of Faust to a "thin string of a single idea" (Goethe to Eckermann, March 6, 1827) is as inadequate as the other extreme of denying the drama's overall unity. The analogy does give us a better understanding of the structure which underlies the total configuration of the *Faust* drama and enriches the meaning of the final lines of the Chorus Mysticus:

> Das Ewig-Weibliche
> Zieht uns hinan.

> Eternal Womanhood
> Leads us above.

NOTES

[1]Cf. Ernst Jockers, "Faust und die Natur," *PMLA* (1947), pp. 436–71.

[2]This assessment of Ernst Jocker's view supersedes my earlier more negative one *(German Quarterly*, May 1966, p. 229). I am glad of the opportunity to correct my error.

[3]Jean-Paul Sartre, *Being and Nothingness*, trans. Hazel E. Barnes (New York, 1956), p. 578.

[4]An important study concerning the imagery and erotic symbolism of moisture and wetness in *Urfaust* is that by R. M. Browning, "On the Structure of the 'Urfaust,'" *PMLA* (1953), pp. 458–95. Many examples cited by Browning apply with equal force to *Faust I*.

[5]The prefigurative aspect of this song was pointed out by R. M. Browning, p. 471.

[6]*Hamb. Ausg.* VIII, p. 320.

[7]Ibid.

[8]Ibid., p. 456.

[9]Ibid. p. 321.

[10]Ibid. I, p. 378.

[11]See Stuart Atkins, *Goethe's Faust, A Literary Analysis* (Cambridge, 1958), p. 139.

[12]For other interpretations in which the key is regarded as a phallic symbol, see Ernst Barthel, *Goethe, das Sinnbild deutscher Kultur* (Darmstadt, 1930), p. 227; Emil Ermatinger, "Goethe und der Mythos," *Die Tatwelt* XI (1935–36), pp. 187–

201; Carl G. Jung, *Symbole der Wandlung*, 4th ed. (Zürich, 1952), p. 208; Robert Lee Wolff, *The Golden Key* (New Haven, 1961), p. 145.

5 • *The "Highest Moment"*

We have now reached a point in our criss-cross journey through *Faust* and Goethe's two scientific works where we may begin to draw the balance of our findings. One can experience the *Faust* drama as an organism without sensing it as metaphor. Goethe could "see" an archetypal plant with his mind's eye and put its "idea" on paper. The *Faust* poem *is* an organism in the sense of a "visible idea," conceived as a form that can be graphically projected. Such projection would again be its visible idea, and so would subsequent projections at the third, fourth, or infinite remove. Nor is there a single correct model that would exclude all others. On the contrary, there is an infinity of correct possibilities which could conceivably stand for the pattern of *Faust*.

This is not to say that *any* scheme would be equally representative. In spite of a multiplicity of possibilities, only those configurations which are held together and activated by the same conjunction of forces could be meaningful symbols or analogies of *Faust*. Within these specifications, however, a series of patterns can be invented. In fact, these patterns should be of such a nature that they hold within them the capacity for infinite variation without detriment to their identity. Goethe's letter to Frau von Stein, written a few months after he came upon the idea of the *Urpflanze*, makes clear the notion of variability within a basic configuration:

> The archetypal plant will be the strangest creature in the world; nature herself shall be envious of it. With this model and the key to it one is in a position to invent an infinity of plants which will have to be consistent with each other, that is to say, even if they do not exist, they yet could exist, not at all as picturesque or poetic shadows but containing an inner truth and necessity. [June 9, 1787]

It is my aim to show that *Faust* has the "inner truth and necessity" of a typical plant conjured up by Goethe's "precise imagination." In a sense, *Faust* is the plant that holds within it all possibilities of the vegetative kingdom. But I have offered in support of my argument not only Goethe's drawing which shows the progressive permutations of the leaf along the stem of a plant (see p. 26), but also the circle and hexagon of colors (p. 31), as well as a diagram representing Faust's development and relationship to surrounding fields of force (see p. 72). In each case we can point to the effective presence of polarity, metamorphosis, heightening and eros. In the area of color, one might cite the interplay of darkness and light which leads to red and beyond it to white by either a positive (yellow) or a negative (blue) route. In Goethe's plant morphology, the play between male and female leads along a spiral path and through a number of transformational stages to a fusion in the pigmented flower.

Goethe's schema in biology naturally approaches more closely the structure of *Faust* than the circle of color, because a plant is a concrete entity and a living organism, whereas color is an attribute without form. The plant, therefore, can be viewed as an enriched version of the circle of color, and, as we shall see, the schema underlying *Faust* is a stupendously expanded and deepened version of the plant.

The peculiar vagueness of objective time in *Faust* which is most apparent in Part II is not of central interest here. The matter has been excellently treated by Herman J. Weigand.[1] What we seek are congruences between the movement of time in Goethe's natural science and the fifty or so years that make up the dramatic time of *Faust*. Let our point of departure be the color circle and let us recall the heightening towards red, which occurs at the "culmination point" *(Theory of Color,* par. 523) and potentially and actually contains all other colors (par. 793). We should also recall that the difficulty of fixing any color at a particular segment of the circle or moment in time increases as one advances toward pure red, whose actual existence occurs only during an infinitely small point in time:

> The mobility of color is so great that even those pigments which you believe to have specified may again be turned one way or the other. [This mobility] is greatest in the vicinity of the culmination point. [Par. 531]

Goethe gives a great deal more attention to the role of time when dealing with plant morphology. Consider the distinction between "progressive" and "regressive" metamorphosis (see p. 24ff). The former has a forward thrust proceeding vigorously step by step from node to stem to leaf, while the latter turns back upon itself, as it were, allowing time for saps to refine themselves, for the leaves to concentrate around a single axis and to transmute into the parts of the flower. This regressive development is characterized by "simultaneity," that is, the sepals, petals, stamens and pistil develop concurrently while the "grosser," progressive development proceeds by successive stages. The color red, like the flower, contains *actu* and *potentia* all previous stages; the simultaneous development of all parts is visible in the flower, though it can be seen only with the spirit's eye in the color red. The plant progresses by expansion and contraction, and the moment of flowering brings with it a diminution by metamorphosis of the basic leaf to form the various parts in the flower. The life force and upward thrust of the plant in bloom have been suspended in favor of concentration and refinement, to prepare for the plant's highest goal, sexual propagation. Goethe uses the botanical term "anastomosis" for this state of concentration and refinement, the interruption of the vital upward thrust, a kind of sleep or symbolic death. Space contracts into a single point (see p. 36) at which length and breadth are annulled (Par. 114). At the end of this stage, the plant resumes its lower functions of growth in the normal expansive manner. We recall that in the color circle red came into being as a result of "darkening" and that its extension in time and space approached zero, corresponding to "concentration" and anastomosis in the plant (see p. 36). Finally, we found that in Goethe's color theory, the red, or any floral color, represents the highest forms of life, which in turn is only a preparation for its transcendence from opacity into "white" or perfect transparency (see p. 37).

The search for a meaningful analogy between the role of time in Goethe's natural science and *Faust* can plausibly begin with the structure and function of the "moment," or the *Augenblick,* which is the subject of the wager between Faust and Mephisto:

> Werd' ich zum Augenblicke sagen:
> Verweile doch! du bist so schön!
> Dann magst du mich in Fesseln schlagen,
> Dann will ich gern zugrunde gehn!
> Dann mag die Totenglocke schallen,
> Dann bist du deines Dienstes frei,
> Die Uhr mag stehn, der Zeiger fallen,
> Es sei die Zeit für mich vorbei!
>
> [1699–1706]

> If ever I should tell the moment:
> O stay! You are so beautiful!
> Then you may cast me into chains,
> then I wish to be annihilated!
> Then may the death bells toll,
> then you are free to leave my service.
> The clock shall halt, the hands shall fall,
> and time be at an end for me!

These lines were among the late additions to *Faust I* and were written after Goethe's Italian journey when he had worked out the main tenets of plant morphology. Certainly the wager concerning the possibility of experiencing the fulfilled moment is most important, if only from the point of view of the unity of the plot. At the end of Part II, the wager had not ceased to be the central issue, and its original terms are repeated almost word for word: "The clock stands still" (l. 11592) says Mephisto, and the chorus of lemurs mumbles in confirmation "Its hands shall fall" (l. 11594). These words appear to mean that Mephisto believes that with his help Faust has indeed experienced the moment to which he can say "Stay! You are so beautiful." Whether or not Faust believes that he has is open to some question and has been the subject of persistent and tenacious debate.[2] The disagreement hinges on Faust's final cunningly subjunctive statement

> Zum Augenblicke dürft ich sagen:
> Verweile doch, du bist so schön!
>
> [11581–82]

> Then to the moment could I say:
> Linger you now, you are so fair!

while surveying with satisfaction his accomplishments as the feudal lord over vast lands peopled by a new, free society.

The fulfilled moment never quite occurs, at least not without hedgings and qualifications. However, foreshadowings of it, or glimpses of the route leading to it, occur in a number of turning points of Faust's dramatic existence. One of these, his union with Helen of Troy, comes closest to meeting all requirements. Even prefigurations and allusions, however, are of interest, because they occur within fairly consistent patterns. An intense concentration on the possibility of "the moment" seems to exert its force on its larger dramatic environment. Thus, what precedes Faust's wager with Mephisto is despair, a brush with suicide and, most immediately, a raging curse directed against all existing values which tumble in an apocalypse of chaos.

> So fluch' ich allem, was die Seele
> Mit Lock- und Gaukelwerk umspannt,
> Und sie in diese Trauerhöhle
> Mit Blend- und Schmeichelkräften bannt!
> Verflucht voraus die hohe Meinung,

Womit der Geist sich selbst umfängt!
Verflucht das Blenden der Erscheinung,
Die sich an unsre Sinne drängt!
Verflucht, was uns in Träumen heuchelt,
Des Ruhms, der Namensdauer Trug!
Verflucht, was als Besitz uns schmeichelt,
Als Weib und Kind, als Knecht und Pflug!
Verflucht sei Mammon, wenn mit Schätzen
Er uns zu kühnen Taten regt,
Wenn er zu müssigem Ergetzen
Die Polster uns zurechtelegt!
Fluch sei dem Balsamsaft der Trauben!
Fluch jener höchsten Liebeshuld!
Fluch sei der Hoffnung! Fluch dem Glauben,
Und Fluch vor allen der Geduld!

[1587–1606]

Now I curse all things that lure my soul
with glittering toys and fantasies
and snare it in this cave of pain
with hocus-pocus and with tinsel bait.
I curse the high opinion
with which the mind deludes itself!
I curse the glare of mere appearance
that presses hard upon our sense!
I curse the whispers of our longing dreams,
the frauds of glory and of lasting fame!
I curse what flatters us as our possessions,
as wife and child or serf and plow!
I curse Mammon and his golden treasures,
inciting us to enterprise
and all his silken cushions
on which to loll in pillowed ease.
My curse upon the balmy sap of grapes!
My curse on lovers' deepest consummation!
My curse on Hope! My curse on Faith,
and cursed be Patience most of all!

Consonant with this denial of life, with the vehemence

and crudeness of Faust's vision at this stage, the "moment" itself is far from what it will be at the end of the drama. Together with other components of the totality of Faust's life, the *Augenblick* itself, which stands at the center of the fable, undergoes successive metamorphoses. Its importance is so great and its power so overwhelming that its mere evocation signals new levels in Faust's development. The *Augenblick* first enters the mainstream of the plot at a time of regression and paralysis. No sooner does Faust emerge from thoughts of suicide—stirred by church bells to memories of childhood and innocence—than the goading prospect of "the moment" transforms him into a man embarked on violent action.

The next allusion to the "moment" occurs in the Witch's Kitchen. A new element in rudimentary form appears: Eros—at its lowest as crass sexuality, and at its highest as service to the ideal of feminine beauty. The Witch's Kitchen was written in Rome in 1788, after Goethe had returned from his trip to Sicily, which had yielded the idea of the archetypal plant. The core of the scene is Faust's rejuvenation by means of the witch's potion. Only a youthful Faust could be a credible lover and experience life as an adventurous quest, free from the weaknesses and disappointed hopes of advanced age. Of special interest in this scene are Faust's words which come suddenly and without apparent connection to the gnomish trappings of the Witch's Kitchen. After having shown first revulsion and then a total lack of interest in the troglodyte goings-on around him, Faust stands transfixed before a mirror, moving sometimes closer, sometimes farther away, trying to fathom the magical image before him. The language rises to a new level, the rhymes (not rendered in this English translation) do not come in subsequent or alter-

nate lines as before, but briefly fall into the more demanding pattern of ABBA. In other words, all signs point to
an unusual and arresting "moment":

> Was seh' ich? Welch ein himmlisch Bild
> Zeigt sich in diesem Zauberspiegel!
> O Liebe, leihe mir den schnellsten deiner Flügel,
> Und führe mich in ihr Gefild!
> Ach! wenn ich nicht auf dieser Stelle bleibe,
> Wenn ich es wage, nah zu gehn,
> Kann ich sie nur als wie im Nebel sehn!—
> Das schönste Bild von einem Weibe!
> Ist's möglich, ist das Weib so schön?
> Muss ich an diesem hingestreckten Leibe
> Den Inbegriff von allen Himmeln sehn?
> So etwas findet sich auf Erden?

[2429–40]

> I see a form of boundless beauty
> give radiance to this magic glass.
> Oh Love, lend me your swiftest wings,
> and lead me to her bright regions.
> Ah, if I try to leave this spot—
> when I dare approach the glass—
> she fades into a cloud of mist.
> Oh, vision of a woman's loveliness!
> Can it be? Can this woman be so fair?
> Do I see in her reclining shape
> the form and essence of the heavens?
> Can this epitome be found on earth?

And as if to emphasize the uniqueness of the vision,
Faust is at cross-purposes with a discomfited Mephisto
when he pleads for another glance at the mirror:

FAUST
> Lass mich nur schnell noch in den Spiegel schauen!
> Das Frauenbild war gar zu schön!

MEPHISTOPHELES

Nein Nein! Du sollst das Muster aller Frauen
Nun bald leibhaftig vor dir sehn.
(leise) Du siehst, mit diesem Trank im Leibe,
Bald Helenen in jeden Weibe.

[2599–2604]

FAUST

Let me quickly look into the glass once more!
The woman's image was so beautiful!

MEPHISTOPHELES

No! No! The paragon of womankind
shall come before you in the flesh.
(Aside) With that potion in your belly
You'll soon see Helena in every wench.

While Faust's "moment" before the glass is still a vague vision, it is richer and more differentiated than the generalized hedonistic *Augenblick* of the wager scene. Mephisto's "You'll soon see Helena in every wench" is a contemptuous cliché, but it is illuminated, as is the vision in the mirror, by the light returned from Faust's still distant future union with Helena. From Mephisto's coldly unpoetic perspective even Helen of Troy is merely another female, but for Faust her spectral appearance provides the first radiance of the "eternal feminine." From this moment on he journeys from carnal lust to "higher consummation." Faust first sees Helena's image *before* drinking the potion, but the decisive effect of the vision becomes evident *after* his transmutation into a young man is complete. It is therefore quite proper to say that Faust's "regression" occurs simultaneously with the experience of "the moment." It is both regression and "darkening," (see p. 36) if one takes into consideration the dimness of the Witch's Kitchen. "The moment" at this stage of the drama also begins to define its temporal structure, for in it Helen of Troy, the Homeric heroine of the distant past, arises as the here-and-now of a vision, and by so doing points to and foreshadows Faust's future. In the satanic abode of the Witch's Kitchen the veiled yet visible idea of Faust's life first arises: a projection in terms of Goethean morphology of the form of the full flower—in almost exact analogy to its botanical counterpart—which will become more real and also more transcendent with each new unfolding.

Nothing else occurs in all the rest of *Faust I* which would qualify as the "moment," while the quest for it continues unabated. In strict adherence to the ancient tradition of magic love potions, Faust is smitten by the first girl who crosses his path. The accidental encounter between the egoistic and insatiable titan and the modest and proper burgher's daughter ends in catastrophe. Yet, Gretchen, by her death and sacrifice, becomes Faust's guiding light. Her simplicity, her unselfish love and instinctive revulsion to evil, prepare Faust for existence at the highest human level. When she dies, Faust dies an inward death lacerated by frustration and guilt. The Faust who is reborn in the second part is a new incarnation whose previous existence has become the meaning and history of its present one.

Certainly "the moment" in Faust's life at the beginning of Part II is a gathering up of the past, a transformation from a limitless hubris to an acceptance of finite and circumscribed human endowment. The images glorify rather than demean life. It is a scene of reflected glory, to be sure, but exquisite during the nightly hours and surpassingly beautiful as the gates are opened to the triumphant light of day crowned by the *Wechseldauer* of the rainbow. Faust is content to drink in this glory even while he is compelled to avert his eyes from the blinding sun. All the same, this is not a moment which provides sufficiency—not a "flower," but perhaps a node in the plant, or a new, more differentiated and more refined leaf. Moreover, it is not a moment of eternity, not a merging of subjective and objective time; rather, Faust is shown outside of and apart from the flow of time. The season is distinctly Spring and as such a beginning rather than a summation. This moment still lacks any reference to eros except in the form of lingering, bitter memories. Benevolent angels hovering over a sleeping Faust chant:

> Besänftiget des Herzens grimmen Strauss,
> Entfernt des Vorwurfs glühend bittre Pfeile,
> Sein Innres reinigt von erlebtem Graus.
>
> [4623–25]

> Soothe now the tumult of this mortal heart,
> And wash away the stain of horrors past;
> Of self-reproach, remove the bitter dart.

Faust is at a relatively "low" point, just as he was at the beginning of the drama, only now on a much higher level of internal development. The "cruder saps" have been refined, growth is no longer rampant, but organized for higher differentiation.

Even at the superior plane on which Faust moves in Part II, the completely fulfilled moment is possible only as a "phantasmagoric" interlude in the third act. There is nothing in *Faust,* probably not in all of Goethe's poetry, to equal the lucid complexity of this act. The opening, written in the famous Greek trimeters,

Bewundert viel und viel gescholten, Helena,
Vom Strande komm' ich, wo wir erst gelandet sind,
[8488–89]

I, Helena, much admired and blamed as much, am come
From yonder shore where newly we have disembarked,

forces the question: who admired and who scolded her?
The Achaians and the Trojans did, to be sure. But
Goethe's Helena refers not only to her appearance in the
Iliad, but also, and perhaps primarily, to the vast stream
of poetry that flowed from her first epic presence into
three millennia of European literature:

Denn seit ich diese Schwelle sorgenlos verliess,

. . . .

Ist viel geschehen, was die Menschen weit and breit
So gern erzählen, aber der nicht gerne hört,
Von dem die Sage wachsend sich zum Märchen spann.
[8510–15]

For since the day I left this threshold, light of heart
. . . .
Full many things have come to pass that, far and near,
The people love to tell, unwelcome talk for one
Of whom the story spread has grown to fabulous tale.

Soon there follows a dialogue during which Phorkias-
Mephisto conjures up erotic episodes from various myths,
in order to burden Helena's conscience with guilt and
despair: her abduction by Theseus when she was a girl
of ten; the "quiet favors" which she had bestowed upon
Patroclus; her unfaithfulness toward her husband Mene-
laus, and her elopement with Paris; the passionate union
of her own shadowy image with that of Achilles who had

116

ascended from Hades. At first the living Helena attempts
to ward off the chimera of her mythical past:

> Verwirre wüsten Sinnes Aberwitz nicht gar.
> Selbst jetzo, welche denn ich sei, ich weiss es nicht.
> [8875–76]

> Spare the confusion in the sad distracted mind.
> Even here, the truth of what I am, I do not know.

and then, as Mephisto presses on, her own concreteness
fades away and recedes into myth:

> Ich als Idol, ihm dem Idol verband ich mich.
> Es war ein Traum, so sagen ja die Worte selbst.
> Ich schwinde hin und werde selbst mir ein Idol.
> [8879–81]

> I, as an idol, joined an idol;
> It was a dream, the gods themselves declare it.
> I fade away and now become an idol to myself.*

At this instant, not only does a sequence of events become
disengaged from temporality, but the dramatic concreteness of the heroine herself is transmuted into the attributes
of her legendary nature. Goethe allows this transcendent
glimpse only for a moment; it occurs during a point of
ignition which fuses past and present, myth and dramatic
reality. The slightest prolongation of such metaphysical
play would allow the mind to see the situation as allegorical or grotesque. One would no longer accept the
action on the stage for its own sake, but react to it much
as one would to a caricature by Saul Steinberg, where an
unfinished emblematic portrait sadly completes its own

*Translation of these three lines is mine.

outline. The idol scene, however, is not humorous but rather one of Goethe's "very serious jokes."[3] While undermining the illusion on the stage, Goethe erects before our inward eye a distilled moment which is concrete and tangible as well as symbolic and universal. In becoming an "idol to herself" Helena has taken herself out of the flow of time and achieved the status of a "visible idea" and of an archetypal phenomenon behind which there is no cause or explanation.

This is also a moment which touches on the limits of poetry. As in the flower there was a telescoping of time into simultaneity, so in this scene Helena's youth and adulthood are fused into one. The merging of experience and legendary history into a single, luminous image is a feat of poetic integration forever denied to science because, in Goethe's words "reason cannot unite what the senses have given . . . in separate units," and denied also to history because its very definition implies successiveness rather than simultaneity. The conflict between idea and experience had always been a challenge to Goethe; only poetry was equal to it. With a touch of irony he spoke of a "convenient escape into poetry" (see p. 19).

Helena "steps out" of herself and is face to face with her emblematic meaning, which is her essence. Under the impact of this self-revelation she faints, continuing then to exist in a dormant state, or symbolic death, from which her emergence signals a new and more highly developed state of being and a readiness for an important turn in the fable. It is only after this moment that Helena meets Faust on an equal footing of dramatic reality. The line "I fade away and now become an idol to myself" indicates a contemplation of self, a narcissistic trance produced by the magical mirrors of poetry which for an instant break her image into its components of myth, meaning, and pure being.

The notion of poetic mirror reflection was not new to Goethe and occurs in somewhat less elaborate form in earlier works. The end of the second chapter of the second part of *Wahlverwandtschaften (Elective Affinities)*, a novel completed in 1808, contains passages from young Ottilie's personal and secret diary, with thoughts of death and speculation on an afterlife:

> Neben denen dereinst zu ruhen, die man liebt, ist die angenehmste Vorstellung, welche der Mensch haben kann. . . . Wenn man die vielen versunkenen . . . Grabsteine . . . erblickt, so kann einem das Leben nach dem Tode doch immer wie ein zweites Leben vorkommen, in das man nun im Bilde, in der Überschrift eintritt und darin länger verweilt als in dem eigentlichen Leben.
>
> [II, 2]

> To rest next to those whom one loves is the most pleasing prospect possible to man. . . . When one looks at the many sunken . . . gravestones . . . , then life after death always seems like a second life into which one enters by way of a picture or an inscription, for a longer sojourn than our life proper.

The following chapter gives an account of the restoration of the interior of a private chapel. A visiting architect, with the help of Ottilie, had adorned the ceiling with frescoes of conventional angels. The architect had completed the work in the course of several weeks during which he had asked Ottilie not to enter it, so that he might surprise her with the beauty of the freshly restored chapel. Probably because he was only an amateur painter lacking in originality, each of the angels' faces turned into a likeness of Ottilie, who had been his companion and helper. When she was finally allowed to enter the chapel her sensation upon seeing her face appear in multiple images on the ceiling is rendered in this remarkable passage:

> Ottilie freute sich der bekannten, ihr als ein unbekanntes Ganze entgegentretenden Teile. Sie stand, ging hin und wieder, sah und besah; endlich setzte sie sich auf einen der Stühle, und es schien ihr, indem sie auf- und umherblickte, als wenn sie wäre und nicht wäre, als wenn sie sich empfände und nicht empfände, als wenn dies alles vor ihr, sie vor sich selbst verschwinden sollte; und nur als die Sonne das bisher sehr lebhaft beschienene Fenster verliess, erwachte Ottilie vor sich selbst und eilte nach dem Schlosse. [II, 3]

> Ottilie was pleased to see the familiar parts which stood before her fused into an unfamiliar whole. She stood still, walked back and forth, saw and observed; in the end she sat down on one of the chairs, and it seemed to her, as she looked up and about, as if she did and did not exist, did and did not perceive herself, as if all those things before her should vanish and she vanish to herself; and only when the sun left the window which until then it had brightly illuminated, did Ottilie awake before her inward self and hurry to the manor.

The parallel between this passage and the idol scene in *Faust* is indisputable, not only in its substance but also in what precedes it: a summing up of experience leading to a drawing together of all powers and a vision of death. As the moment of "doubling" prepared Helena for her phantasmagoric union with Faust, so Ottilie's similar experience is the signal for a new state of her being which

leads to her resolve henceforth to love Eduard disin-
terestedly and which prepares her for a higher or transcendent consummation of their passion.

In *Elective Affinities,* as well as in *Faust,* the model
for the poetic vision of double mirror images is present
in Goethe's natural philosophy. It is inherent in the
"anastomosis" of the plant, in the color red of the circle,
and more specifically in Goethe's tract on "Entoptic
Colors" written in 1820 as an addition to and elaboration
of *Theory of Color.* He had already treated the phenomenon of double images under the rubric of "physical
colors," and now with the availability of new experiments
on polarization in France conducted in 1809 and subsequent speculations by his friend Seebeck he felt ready
to write an extensive tract on the subject. These experiments dealt with the double or multiple images resulting
from light refracted through mica, selenite, and feldspar.
Under paragraph 29 we read:

> Herein we find another magnificent example of how
> all things are ultimately interconnected, related to one
> another and responsive to each other. What happens in
> the air about us occurs also in the human eye, and
> the entoptic opposition is also a physiological one . . .
> thus the object—without regard to its relative darkness
> or brightness—will, like a ghostly image, stand reversed
> in the eye. . . .[4]

Goethe's fondness for mirror images as phenomena in
the natural world and their counterparts in life and literature can easily be documented. For instance, a short
autobiographical note written in 1822 and published
posthumously was inspired by an account of a friend's
visit to Sesenheim, the place where the young Goethe met

and loved Friederike Brion. The concluding paragraph contains this:

> If we consider that repeated moral reflections not only keep the past alive, but even intensify it to a higher life, then we will be mindful of the entoptic images which also by no means diminish from mirror to mirror but flash out all the more, then we will acquire a symbol for events which in the histories of the arts and religion—and probably in the political sphere as well—have occurred repeatedly and are still occurring every day.[5]

The word "ghostly" (*gespenstig*) appearing in the first quotation is used to characterize the reflected entoptic image and occurs in other accounts of the same phenomenon. The reference to the past and present in the last quotation, and the explicit mention of the symbolic significance of mirror reflections places the Ottilie episode, as well as the idol scene in the third act of *Faust,* into the proper relationship with Goethe's natural science. We must be careful, however, not to look upon Goethe's use of scientific methods for literary purposes as a device, but rather as evidence of the essential unity of his outlook. To him a truth in natural science was also a truth in art.

Inasmuch as the center of the "moment" we are discussing is occupied by Helen of Troy, it contains all aspects of feminity, from irresistible guile to serene aesthetic perfection. The substance, history, meaning, and form of this "moment" are at once available to a heightened spiritual capacity (see p. 14). But at this juncture it is still only Helena's moment, not Faust's. For him the unity between the old and the new is yet to be established. Greek antiquity and the modern romantic spirit must

be merged. In the presence of the strange northern knight,
Helena, who had spoken in classical trimeters, gradually
adjusts her speech to Faust's iambic rhythms, and in a
foreshadowing of their union lovingly responds to Faust,
in un-Grecian rhymes:

HELENA
   So sage denn, wie sprech' ich auch so schön?
FAUST
   Das ist gar leicht, es muss von Herzen gehn.
   Und wenn die Brust von Sehnsucht überfliesst,
   Man sieht sich um und fragt—
HELENA

                . . . wer mitgeniesst

FAUST
   Nun schaut der Geist nicht vorwärts, nicht zurück,
   Die Gegenwart allein—
HELENA

         . . . ist unser Glück.

                    [9377–83]

HELENA
   For words so lovely, how the gift impart?
FAUST
   Soon said: it must come welling from the heart;
   And, overflows heart's bliss without alloy,
   We lift our eyes and ask—
HELENA

        Who shares the joy?

FAUST
   Then not to past or future turns the mind,
   And only in the present—
HELENA

       Bliss we find.

The "idol" scene is the final preparation for this blissful
union. More and more opposites are now drawn into an

operatic gesture of joy. The fusion of time and space
which had occurred even before Faust's entrance is enriched and made concrete by the union of male and
female, classical man and modern man, Greek meter and
northern rhymes. It is also possible to regard the idol
scene and the union between Faust and Helena jointly
as a single pair of "moments," like a cluster of blossoms
which one finds in certain plants and is seen as a double
or multiple flowering, preceded by the most elaborate
regression, or symbolic death.

Late in the first act of Part II, Faust prepares to descend
to the realm of the Mothers. A reluctant Mephisto alludes
to their habitat by mystifying and confusing directions:

FAUST:
    Wohin der Weg?
MEPHISTO:

                    Kein Weg! Ins Unbetretene,
    Nicht zu Betretende; ein Weg in Unerbetene,
    Nicht zu Erbittende. Bist du bereit?—

[6222–25]

FAUST:
    Where lies the way?
MEPHISTO:
    There is none. Way to the Unreachable,
    Never for treading, to those Unbeseechable,
    Never besought! Is your soul then ready?

This Mephistophelian mystification reminds Faust of a
moment in the distant past:

    Du spartest, dächt' ich, solche Sprüche;
    Hier wittert's nach der Hexenküche,
    Nach einer längst vergangnen Zeit.

[6228–30]

124

> You could dispense with speeches of this kind,
> Which bring the Witch's Kitchen back to mind,
> An echo of far distant days renewed.

The witch's mumbo-jumbo of long ago has become the solemn contradictory assertion pronounced in an only slightly hidden two-beat hymnic rhythm of previous and subsequent angelic choirs.[6] Mephistopheles' speech is affected by the profundity of its meaning and warped into momentary solemnity. Even regression, therefore, is transmuted into higher significance. The witch's realm has now become the formative matrix, the *ur*-norm of still unformed being, and as such surrounded by allusions to its dwelling place beyond comprehension, as well as to its sacredness. The descent to the Mothers is Faust's most dangerous adventure, a journey into non-being, which causes concern even to Mephisto: "I wonder if he ever will return" (1. 6306). Faust finally does emerge, bringing with him Helena's spectral form, but he is struck unconscious during the reenactment of her legend. He awakens from the death-like sleep in which he lies only after he is transported through time and space to the scene of the Classical Walpurgis Night on the Pharsalian Fields. As Mephisto and Homunculus set him down on Greek soil so that he may find the "real" Helena in Hades, he exclaims, seemingly out of context, "Where is she?" During the rest of the second act we hear or see nothing of Faust or Helena for about a thousand lines of text during which the Classical Walpurgis Night unfolds in an elaborate oceanic festival. Only the third act finally shows Helena in full dramatic concreteness, in preparation for her en-, counter with a medieval lord named Faust. A new metamorphosis has been effected and the "highest consummation" between polar opposites is about to take place. Goethe called the entire third act "eine Phantas-magorie," and we can see it as a series of fantastic, though symbolically coherent, events.

If the third act were regarded as part of the plot in the ordinary sense, it would look as though either Goethe or Mephisto "nodded" during Faust's union with Helena. Would this not be the "moment" which was the subject of the wager? Faust does not flee from it as he had fled from permanent involvement with Gretchen. Now it is Helena who vanishes, before her union with Faust is demeaned by the stultifying effects of chronological time and human limits. If, in the light of the Helena episode, we consider Faust's words of long ago, accompanying the wager with Mephisto:

> Werd' ich zum Augenblicke sagen:
> Verweile doch! du bist so schön!
> Dann magst Du mich in Fesseln schlagen,
> Dann will ich gern zugrunde gehn!
>
> [1699–1702]

> If ever I should tell the moment:
> O stay! You are so beautiful!
> Then you may cast me into chains,
> then I wish to be annihilated!

then the question of Faust's alliance with the devil takes on special significance: Faust's yearning is so absolute, and his disillusionment with life so radical, that he is willing to stake everything on his conviction that even hell cannot give him what he so desperately seeks, the absolute and timeless moment. When in poetry and myth he is united with Helena over three millennia of history he clings to the luminous instant with all his strength. The wager with Mephisto, therefore, is profoundly paradoxical because Faust actually longs to lose it. When he says:

> Die Uhr mag stehn, der Zeiger fallen,
> Es sei die Zeit für mich vorbei!
>
> [1703–05]
>
> The clock shall halt, the hands shall fall,
> and time be at an end for me!

he is alluding to the condition of damnation in the tradition of the Faust legend, but also evoking and foreshadowing the perfect moment which lies beyond the grasp of the rationalist and unpoetic Mephisto. Hence Faust's "Then you are free to leave my service" (1. 1704). And because such a moment would be above and beyond time, he can say "The clock shall halt, the hands shall fall," and be content to die.

Why then does Mephisto not intervene when Faust and Helena are united?[7] As we have seen, the union is an utterly fulfilled moment which should make it easy for Mephisto to claim his wage. It would be a mistake to conclude, as Wilhelm Emrich does,[8] that the *Augenblick* as envisioned here is qualitatively so different from the one which was the subject of the wager between Faust and Mephisto, that they are in fact not significantly related. The growth of the "moment" through a number of metamorphoses is clear enough now; its evolution by no means cancels its identity. The reason for the absence of Mephistophelean intervention in the third act of *Faust II* must be sought in the mythical and phantasmagoric quality of the union between Faust and Helena. The experience with Helen of Troy does not properly touch

Faust as an historical being, for Mephisto's intended victim must be fully human and confined within the limits of time. That is clear from Mephisto's dialogue with the Lord in the "Prologue in Heaven."

In the last act, Faust finally appears to experience the supreme moment while engaged in a practical down-to-earth enterprise—the accretion and cultivation of coastal lands. At this point he becomes subject to the terms of the contract. But in losing his bet with the devil, Faust does not go to hell; he has earned the right to Divine Grace.

Faust's death and ascension constitute the final and transcendent metamorphosis. In the one hundred years of his life, he has learned to live as an historical being. No longer does he seek to invade the realm of the absolute or of omniscience by incantation or magic. He has found that ceaseless human activity can provide at least a relative kind of permanence.

> Es kann die Spur von meinen Erdentagen
> Nicht in Äonen untergehn.—
>
> [11583–84]
>
> Now records of my earthly day
> No flight of aeons can impair.—

Faust has stopped dreaming and stopped "associating himself with a poet." His human frailty is brought home to him when he is struck blind, but this additional impediment is brushed aside with a renewed commitment to the task at hand:

> FAUST (erblindet)
> Die Nacht scheint tiefer tief hereinzudringen,
> Allein im Innern leuchtet helles Licht;

> Was ich gedacht, ich eil' es zu vollbringen;
> Des Herren Wort, es gibt allein Gewicht.
>
> . . . .
>
> Dass sich das grosse Werk vollende,
> Genügt ein Geist für tausend Hände.
>
> [11499–510]

FAUST (blinded)
> Deep falls the night, in gloom precipitate;
> What then? Clear light within my mind shines still;
> Only the master's word gives action weight,
> And what I framed in thought I will fulfill.
>
> . . . .
>
> To end the greatest work designed,
> A thousand hands need but one mind.

Ironically, the great task to be completed is the digging of Faust's grave. Faust is deceived about the scope and purpose of the works he has set in motion. A draining ditch is in reality a small excavation for a body of average size, and all the gigantic projects wrought by an obedient people are subject to decay and obliteration.

Faust's yearned-for *Augenblick* which occurs at the point of his death signals fulfillment only for him. To an objective observer the deception must be clear; the grandeur of the scene holds within it a confirmation of the futility of life. But Goethe bestows Divine Grace on Faust's soul even when it is deceived. From an ultimate perspective, the deception is itself a deception.

In the sphere of timelessness, which in the final scene takes the form of the Catholic heaven, Faust's earthly life appears in retrospect as a chrysalis and a sleep. The "Choir of Blessed Boys" chants:

> Freudig empfangen wir
> Diesen im Puppenstand;

. . . .
Löset die Flocken los,
Die ihn umgeben!

[11981–86]

Him as soul's chrysalis
Joyful receive we;

. . . .
Shake off the earthly flakes
That yet enfold him;

As his soul is carried to ever higher and purer regions, it approaches the spirit of Gretchen. *Una poenitentiarum,* closely resembling Dante's Beatrice, becomes his guide in heaven. Once in deepest pain and distress Gretchen had prayed to the *mater dolorosa,* the sacred image of Mary set in recess of the town wall:

Ach neige,
Du Schmerzenreiche,
Dein Antlitz gnädig meiner Not!

Das Schwert im Herzen,
Mit tausend Schmerzen
Blickst auf zu deines Sohnes Tod.

[3586–92]

Incline
Oh Merciful,
Thy grieving countenance to my grief!

With sword in heart—
A thousandfold wound—
Thy gaze rests on his death.

Now, in close proximity to Mary's heavenly sphere, the prayer is transmuted into a hymn of thanksgiving:

Neige, neige
Du Ohnegleiche,
Du Strahlenreiche,
Dein Antlitz gnädig meinem Glück!
Der früh Geliebte,
Nicht mehr Getrübte,
Er kommt zurück.

[12069–75]

Incline, incline,
Thou matchless one,
Thou radiant one,
Thy gracious countenance to my bliss.
The early beloved,
No longer dimmed,
Comes back to me now.*

Faust has reached the greatest fulfillment by existing in an eternal present. And so has the drama. The last scene is the "highest consummation," the flowering that occurs after a death, and has greater finality than previous intimations of dying. It carries the highest symbolic meaning both *actu* and *potentia,* including the essence of medieval Catholic dogma.

*Translation is mine.

NOTES

[1]"Goethe's *Faust,* An Introduction for Students and Teachers of General Literature," Part I, *The German Quarterly* (November 1964), pp. 467–86; Part II, (January, 1965), pp. 1–13.

[2]See, for example: Ada Klett, *Der Streit um Faust II seit 1900* (Jena, 1939); Harry Steinhauer, "Faust's Pact with the Devil," *PMLA* (March, 1956), pp. 180–200; Hermann Weigand, "Wetten und Pakt in Goethes *Faust,*" *Monatshefte* (December, 1961), pp. 325–37.

[3]See, for example, his letter to Wilhelm von Humboldt of March 7, 1832.

[4]*Weimarer Ausgabe*, Abt. II, vol. 5_1, p. 293.

[5]*Jubiläums.* XXV, pp. 222–23.

[6]See, for example, Part I:

> Christ ist erstanden!
> Freude dem Sterblichen,
> Den die Verderblichen,
> Schleichenden, erblichen
> Mängel umwanden.
>
> [737–41]

or Part II:

> Rosen, ihr blendenden
> Balsam versendenden!
> Flatternde, schwebende,
> Heimlich belebende,
> Zweiglein beflügelte,
> Knospenentsiegelte,
> Eilet zu blühn.
>
> [11699–705]

[7]For a recent discussion of this problem, see Hermann Weigand "Wetten und Pakte in Goethes *Faust*," *Monatshefte* (December, 1961), p. 337.

[8]"Nichts aber wäre widergoethescher, als die Feier des Augenblicks' mit Fausts Wette in Verbindung bringen zu wollen. . . ." (Wilheim Emrich, *Die Symbolik von Faust II* [Bonn, 1957], p. 343.)

Summation

Scholarship moves on thin ice when it resorts to metaphors and analogies in explicating poetic images. On the face of it this practice would appear to be compounding the difficulties of interpretation by interposing yet another obstacle between the reader and the material he aims to understand. The separation between the genres of critical analysis and creative writing has often been held to be inviolable, and the epithet "belletristic" has become a term of opprobium used to castigate any departure from a rigorously cognitive approach to literary criticism.

Yet the fruitfulness of adjusting one's critical perceptions and articulations to the literary work under scrutiny has become evident to me in no little measure in the course of this study. Inasmuch as Goethe insisted that to a delicately empirical mind the theory behind the phenomenon is the phenomenon itself, we might meet him on those terms and be unashamed in responding to the *Faust* poem with all our faculties, rather than forcing our sympathetic vibrations through the selective filter of a rigorous cerebral and syllogistic analysis. Goethe fought long and hard against the application of logical and mathematical categories to living nature, and he thought that the best literary works belong to the order of complex organisms. The analogy between nature and literary art in Goethe's mind must be regarded as given, since it demonstrably colored so much of his imaginative and scientific writings. To deny its relevance to *Faust* criticism is bound to deaden a whole range of valid responses to it. Critical illumination, after all, need not restrict itself entirely to cognitive analysis. It is only after we arrange and readjust our own impulses that we move toward a capacity for hearing the authentic voice over its entire range. "You're like the Spirit that you grasp," Goethe has the Earth Spirit say to Faust, who cannot stand up to the apparition—much less understand it—because he does not in any way resemble it, at least not yet. Echoing Plotinus, the verses inserted in the Introduction to the *Theory of Color* similarly stress the necessity of kinship between the observer and nature as a precondition to "seeing":

> Wär nicht das Auge sonnenhaft,
> Wie könnten wir das Licht erblicken?
> Lebt nicht in uns des Gottes eigne Kraft,
> Wie könnt' uns Göttliches entzücken?[1]

> If eyes resembled not the sun
> How could we countenance the Light?
> If God's own power did not live within,
> How could divinity enthrall us?

We are of course under no obligation to model ourselves on Goethe in order to interpret his *Faust* poem, but we will not lose anything by provisionally accepting some of his basic tenets. These are not irrelevant principles brought in from outside the framework of the poem. I think that they have been shown to reside near its core, for Goethe's philosophy of nature is, in a sense, his aesthetic philosophy as well. Even after each scene and verse are analyzed as verbal configurations—which they irrevocably are—there remains the *geistige Band,* the spiritual web, which may so easily slip through our fingers.

In the case of this study the attempt to locate a basic impulse that permeates the *Faust* poem has led to the elaboration of an organic analogy—specifically of the plant. The predilection in the late eighteenth century for metaphors of growth and vegetative life is well documented. In 1759, E. Young in his *Conjectures on Original Composition* wrote: "An original may be said to be of vegetable nature; it rises spontaneously from the vital root of genius; it grows, it is not made,"[2] The book had an immediate impact in Germany where two separate translations appeared before the end of 1761. For the writers of the Storm and Stress movement the *Conjectures* was as much a primary theoretical document as the colossal and nebulous figure of Shakespeare had become a realization and paradigm of genius. Goethe was a member of this strident and rebellious group of Stormers and Stressers. Titanism and vehement eroticism were their stock in trade, with an admixture of anti-Establishment protest and Rousseauistic nature worship. Among the most fateful Storm and Stress themes that found their way into Goethe's *Faust* was the story behind the Gretchen episode. Its raw material—a legal case of some notoriety at the time—is the seduction and abandonment of a simple burgher's daughter by her unscrupulous lover. Driven to despair by public opprobium she becomes the murderess of her illegitimate child. What had been a social protest against the inhumanity of established law on infanticide became in the hands of Goethe a dramatization of a demonic and transcendent passion. The delicate natural and social balance surrounding the Gretchen of the drama becomes upset, and catastrophe is the inevitable result. In works such as *Werther,* a balance could be restored only through the protagonist's death. In *Wilhelm Meisters Wanderjahre,* Felix's impetuous embrace of Hersilie also ends in catastrophe (see p. 99). Only Faust, the self-centered titan, is able to absorb disaster and is fully restored to nature through healing sleep, but only after Gretchen has assumed all guilt by her sacrifice.

In the end, Faust's natural death and his salvation ought to be sufficient to exclude him from the category of tragic heroes cast in the Aristotelean mold. But there are other, perhaps more telling, reasons that militate against a "tragic" reading of *Faust.* There is no nemesis, for example, no Sophoclean cosmic meat grinder oiled and fueled by human sacrifice. Mephisto is too involved in Faust's person and represents too transparent a principle to qualify as an emissary of unfathomable Fate. Also, he functions at the pleasure of the Lord, and only so long as his devilish schemes ultimately "effect the good." Unlike Greek fate, the Goethean devil is an eschatologically subalternate power. Even if Mephisto had succeeded in toppling Faust from his titanic aspirations, the play would not be a "tragedy." The Aristotelian premises are absent. As Erich Heller points out: "There is no catharsis—only metamorphoses."[3]

Connected with this is the absence of a sense of tragic guilt. In *Faust* and in almost all other dramatic works of Goethe, a sense of guilt does not result from a free choice between two clear-cut alternatives, but is a steady concomitant of human consciousness. Friedrich Gundolf in his biography of Goethe in 1916 wrote:

> Man attains to an inward law, an inborn natural norm, like the plant, only with man this norm is conscious . . . its violation, therefore, regardless of whether committed carelessly or under compulsion, constitutes guilt. Unconscious nature knows no guilt. . . .[4]

Guilt is a deviation from nature, an excess or a stagnation, and to Goethe a sickness rather than a moral category. Tragedy is the "sickness unto death" of Werther, and Goethe's avoidance of tragedy is also a defensive stance against a return to the Wertherian malaise. The long list of Faust's misdeeds—the killing of Gretchen's brother Valentin, his part in the death of Gretchen's mother and illegitimate child, his abandonment of her in the dungeon, and his complicity, toward the end of the drama, in the death of Philemon and Baucis—are all concomitants of his ruthless quest for the ambivalent boon of "knowledge." But as is the case with Adam and Eve and with Oedipus, knowledge and self-consciousness reveal guilt, and when both consciousness and self, in terms of striving and activity, are heightened and intensified, so is the guilt made more devastating. Only a kind of death, or sleep, or "regression" can effect a return to the innocence of nature and prepare for a higher metamorphosis. Aristotle's criteria for tragedy simply do not apply to *Faust*. Goethe's subtitle "eine Tragödie" refers to the tragedy of being human, to the inability to expand the concrete human reality to a point where it would match the vision of a metaphysical absolute, cleansed of such indirections and ambiguities as similies, metaphors, and polarities.

On the other hand, the structural principles embodied in *Faust* are remarkably analogous to those of Goethe's paradigmatic plant, and only slightly less so, of the circle of color. Erich Heller writes in his essay "Goethe and the Avoidance of Tragedy":

> When the crisis is over, the heroes are at one again with the spirit of Nature. They are not purified in the tragic sense, not raised above their guilt through atonement, but enter, as it were, a biologically, or morally, new sphere of life, healed by oblivion and restored to strength through the sleep of the just.[5]

This insight seems to me to give sanction to what has here been attempted: a demonstration of the essential identity, in terms of his works, between Goethe as a natural philosopher and as a poet. The poet's imagination, which could integrate the archetypal phenomena of polarity, metamorphosis, and heightening, was capable of creating *Faust* in the image of the "Plant."

Through his youthful preoccupation with alchemy and the mysticism of Jacob Böhme, and his knowledge of Giordano Bruno's neo-platonism, Goethe had come to oppose the Cartesian mechanistic world view of which Isaac Newton was a prime representative.[6] Leibnitz's monads, the "perpetual living mirrors of the universe," as well as several passages in Shaftesbury, served to enrich and modify for Goethe the nature worship inherent in Schelling's *Naturphilosophie* and the Rousseauistic leanings of his friend and tutor Herder. During the eighteenth century, the "organistic" world view among German poets and philosophers alike had gradually replaced the Cartesian and Newtonian conception of the universe. This was a way to conceive of a soul, or an active center that animates the whole of nature. It was also a pious attitude compatible with a pantheistic religious philosophy that viewed man as exposed to and permeated by divinity. Rather than merely allowing his poetry to be infused by the new nature worship, Goethe avidly cast his mind and soul into the concreteness of his environment in order to find scientific confirmation for his intuitive and emotional grasp of nature. Thus he conceived the archetypal plant actually some time before it was "revealed" to him in the public gardens of Palermo.[7] Ronald Gray has shown how Goethe's youthful studies and experiments in alchemy had conditioned him to view the growth of a plant as a heightening process culminating in the blossom and the act of sexual reproduction, and how these same studies had taught him to organize color phenomena according to analogous principles.[8] Although the mature Goethe rejected alchemy and its associated mysticism as false and even dangerous, he was profoundly influenced by its symbols, which expressed to him permanent human yearnings and "self-revealing mysteries."

For these reasons the analogies existing between Goethe's *Faust* and the processes of nature indicate much more than an adherence to fashion and more than a new departure in poetic diction, though these are noteworthy in themselves. The dynamics of the *Faust* poem, its movement from crude hedonism to the sublimity of the perfect moment, partake of the actuality of Goethe's natural philosophy. The analogy is remarkably precise though it cannot be expected to resolve specific textual problems in *Faust*.

Goethe was well aware that his poem would have to wait a long time before it could evoke widespread sympathy and understanding. During his last period of creativity he consistently referred to *Faust* as the "main business" *(Hauptgeschäft)* of his remaining days. To his composer friend Zelter he wrote:

> It is no trifling thing, at the age of eighty-two, to render concretely real a matter that was originally conceived at twenty . . . so that everything may remain a self-revealing mystery and people may time and again ponder over it and derive pleasure from it. [June 1, 1831]

His amanuensis Eckermann reported how profoundly happy Goethe was that it should have been given to him to complete his poem: "From now on," Eckermann quotes him as saying, "I can regard my life as a pure gift, and it really doesn't matter what I still may and may not do" (June 6, 1831). On September 7 he sealed up the manuscript, for it was his wish that it should not be opened during his lifetime.[9] In the last letter dealing with *Faust*, he wrote to his old friend Wilhelm v. Humboldt:

> But our age is so . . . confused, I have become convinced that my honest and long-continued efforts with respect to this strange edifice would be poorly rewarded and lie about stranded and ruined like a derelict vessel to be buried for some time by the debris and sand of the hours. [March 17, 1832]

NOTES

[1]Cf. p. 79; see also Plotinus, *Enneads* V, 8, 1.
[2]*Conjectures on Original Composition*, ed. E. K. Morley (Manchester, 1918), p. 8. See also pp. 11, 13–15.
[3]*The Disinherited Mind* (New York, 1959), p. 60.
[4]*Goethe* (Berlin, 1920), p. 147.

[5]Op. cit., p. 60.

[6]See Harold Jantz, *Goethe's Faust as a Renaissance Man* (Princeton, 1951); Ronald Gray, *Goethe the Alchemist* (Cambridge, 1952); Werner Saenger, "Goethe and Giordano Bruno," *Germanische Studien,* (Berlin, 1930), Heft 91; J. Richter, "Jacob Böhme and Goethe," *Jahrbuch des freien deutschen Hochstifts* (1934–35).

[7]See pp. 7, 105.

[8]*Goethe the Alchemist* (Cambridge 1952), pp. 54–100.

[9]Letter to Graf Reinhard (September 7, 1831).

Bibliography

Arber, Agnes. "Goethe's Botany." *Chronica Botanica* X:2 (1946).

Atkins, Stuart. *Goethe's Faust, A Literary Analysis.* Cambridge, 1958.

______."The Interpretation of Goethe's *Faust* Since 1958." *Orbis Litterarum* XX (1965), pp. 239–67.

______."Studies of Goethe's *Faust* Since 1959." *The German Quarterly* XXXIX (May, 1966), pp. 303–10. This is a resumé of the article by the same author in *Orbis Litterarum.*

Bacon, Francis. *The Advancement of Learning,* G. W. Kitchin, ed. London, 1915.

Bahr, Ehrhard. ". . . diese sehr ernsten Scherze . . . ." *Jahrbuch der Goethe-Gesellschaft* XXXI (1969), pp. 157–73.

Barthel, Ernst. *Goethe, das Sinnbild deutscher Kultur.* Darmstadt, 1930.

Bernays, Adolph. "Zur Frage des Lichtsinns." *Dialectica* (October, 1949), pp. 236–41.

Browning, R. M. "On the Structure of the *Urfaust.*" *PMLA* (1953), pp. 458–95.

Cassirer, Ernst. *The Problem of Knowledge, Philosophy and Science Since Hegel.* New Haven, 1950.

Emrich, Wilhelm. *Die Symbolik von Faust II.* Bonn, 1957.

Fähnrich, Hermann. "Goethes Musikanschauung in seiner Fausttragödie—die Erfüllung und Vollendung seiner Opernreform." *Jahrbuch der Goethe-Gesellschaft* XXV (1963), pp. 250–63.

Gillispie, Charles C. *The Edge of Objectivity: An Essay in the History of Scientific Ideas.* Princeton, 1960.

Gray, Ronald. *Goethe the Alchemist.* Cambridge, 1962.

Gundolf, Friedrich. *Goethe.* Berlin, 1920.

Heisenberg, Werner. "Das Naturbild Goethes und die technischnaturwissenschaftliche Welt." *Jahrbuch der Goethe-Gesellschaft* XXIX (1967), pp. 27–42.

———. "Die Goethische und Newtonsche Farbenlehre im Lichte der Modernen Physik." *Geist der Zeit* XIX: 5 (May, 1941), pp. 268–70.

———. *Wandlungen in den Grundlagen der Naturwissenschaft.* Zurich, 1947.

Heller, Erich. *The Disinherited Mind.* New York, 1959.

Henel, Heinrich. "Goethe und die Naturwissenschaft." *Journal of English and German Philology* XLVIII (1949), pp. 507–32.

———. "Type and Proto-Phenomenon in Goethe's Science." *PMLA* (1956), pp. 651–68.

Herz, Wilhelm. *Goethes Naturphilosophie in Faust.* Berlin, 1913.

———. *Natur und Geist in Goethes Faust.* Frankfurt, 1931.

Jantz, Harold. *Goethe's Faust as a Renaissance Man.* Princeton, 1951.

Jockers, Ernst. "Faust und die Natur." *PMLA* (1947), pp. 436–71.

———. "Morphologie und Klassik Goethes." *Goethe und die Wissenschaft.* Frankfurt/M., 1951.

Jung, Carl G. *Symbole der Wandlung,* 4th ed. Zurich, 1952.

Klett, Ada. *Der Streit um Faust II seit 1900.* Jena, 1939.

Korff, Karl A. *Geist der Goethezeit,* 2nd ed. Leipzig, 1954.

Land, Edwin H. "Experiments in Color Vision." *Scientific American* (May, 1959), pp. 84–99.

Lavater, Joh. Caspar. *Physiognomische Fragmente zur Beförderung der Menschenkenntnis und Menschenliebe.* Leipzig and Winterthur, 1775–78.

Mann, Thomas. *Essays of Three Decades,* tr. H. T. Lowe-Porter. New York, 1947.

Müller, Günther. "Die Gestaltfrage in der Literaturwissenschaft and Goethes Morphologie." *Die Gestalt*, Heft 13. Halle, 1964.

Naef, Adolf. *Idealistische Morphologie und Philogenetik. Zur Methode der systematischen Morphologie.* Jena, 1919.

Nicolson, Marjorie Hope. *The Breaking of the Circle.* Evanston, Ill., 1950.

Oppel, Horst. *Morphologische Naturwissenschaft. Goethes Ansicht und Methode.* Mainz, 1947.

Politzer, Heinz. "The Tree of Knowledge and the Sin of Science: Vegetation Symbols in Goethe's Faust." *Aspects of the Eighteenth Century*, Earl R. Wasserman, ed. Baltimore, 1965, pp. 281–304.

Radl, E. *Geschichte der biologischen Theorien in de Neuzeit.* Leipzig, 1909.

Rehder, Helmut. "Tetradic Structure in Goethe's *Faust.*" *The Germanic Review* XXXVIII (January, 1963), pp. 52–65.

Richter, J. "Jacob Böhme und Goethe." *Jahrbuch des freien deutschen Hochstifts* (1934–35).

Saenger, Werner. "Goethe und Giordano Bruno." *Germanische Studien*, Heft 91. Berlin, 1930.

Salm, Peter. "Faust, Eros and Knowledge." *The German Quarterly* (May, 1966), pp. 329–39.

———. "Faust and Irony." *Germanic Review* (May, 1965, pp. 192–204.

Santayana, George. *Three Philosophical Poets*, 8th ed. Cambridge, 1947.

Sartre, Jean-Paul. *Being and Nothingness*, tr. Hazel E. Barnes. New York, 1956.

Sherrington, Charles. *Goethe on Nature and Science*, 2nd ed. Cambridge, 1949.

Steinhauer, Harry. "Faust's Pact with the Devil." *PMLA* (March, 1956), pp. 180–200.

Wachsmuth, Andreas B. "Goethes Farbenlehre und ihre Bedeutung für seine Dichtung und Weltanschauung." *Jahrbuch der Goethe-Gesellschaft* XXI (1959), pp. 70–93.

Weigand, Herman J. "Goethe's *Faust*, An Introduction for Students and Teachers of General Literature." Part I, *The German Quarterly* (November, 1964), pp. 467–86; Part II (January, 1965), pp. 1–13.

————. "Wetten und Pakt in Goethes *Faust*." *Monatshefte* (December, 1961), pp. 325–37.

Wilkinson, Elizabeth M., and L. A. Willoughby. *Goethe, Poet and Thinker*. New York, 1962.

Wimsatt, W. K. *The Verbal Icon, Studies in the Meaning of Poetry*, 2nd ed. New York, 1958.

Wolff, Robert L. *The Golden Key*. New Haven, 1961.

Young, Edward. *Conjectures on Original Composition*, ed. E. K. Morley. Manchester, 1918.

CONSULTED EDITIONS OF GOETHE'S WRITINGS

Hamburger Ausgabe, ed. Eric Trunz, 14 vols., 3rd. ed. Hamburg, 1956; also in this edition, *Goethes Briefe*, ed. K. R. Mandelkow and B. Morawe, 4 vols. Hamburg, 1962.

Jubiläumsausgabe, ed. E. v. d. Hellen, 40 vols. Stuttgart and Berlin, 1902–12.

Weimarer Ausgabe, 143 vols. Weimar, 1887–1919.

Gedenkausgabe, ed. Ernst Beutler, 24 vols. Zurich, 1948–50.

GOETHE'S CONVERSATIONS

Goethes Gespräche, ed. F. Frhr. v. Biedermann, 5 vols., 2nd ed. Leipzig, 1909–11.

PUBLISHED TRANSLATIONS USED

Faust I, tr. Peter Salm. New York: Bantam Books, 1967.

Faust II, tr. Philip Wayne. Baltimore: Penguin Books, 1959.

Iphigenia, tr. Anna Swanwick. Philadelphia, n.d.

Tasso, tr. Ben Kimpel and T. C. Duncan Eaves. Fayetteville, Ark., 1956.

Index